Intimate Conversations With God

52 Weeks of Thought Provoking Devotionals

Roxanne Gail Hodge

INTIMATE CONVERSATIONS WITH GOD

First Edition, January 22, 2023

Copyright @2023 Roxanne Gail Hodge

ISBN: 979-8215179253

Written by Roxanne Gail Hodge

Introduction

THE God of the universe is a God of relationships. I get overwhelmed when I think about the goodness of His love and the magnitude of the power that comes with His love. It was years before I fully embraced how much my Heavenly Father loves me. Never were truer words spoken than the observation Paul made in Ephesians.

Ephesians 3:17-19 (NLT)

17 Then Christ will make his home in your hearts as you trust in him. Your roots will grow down into God's love and keep you strong. 18 And may you have the power to understand, as all God's people should, how wide, how long, how high, and how deep his love is. 19 May you experience the love of Christ, though it is too great to understand fully. Then you will be made complete with all the fullness of life and power that comes from God.

I'm convinced prayer is a mystery to believers. Often, when there is a difficult concept to embrace, people create tools to simplify their understanding. Such as we have done with prayer. To explain what prayer is, we have created a one-size-fits-all formula. The truth is prayer is merely conversations with God.

Do we talk to each person we know the same way? No, we don't. God wants us to speak to Him, and He wants to respond. When become more acquainted with the Father, we are more comfortable talking to Him, and the more we hear Him, the more we understand His Words.

This devotional book INTIMATE CONVERSATIONS WITH GOD is meant to share how plainly and simply The Holy Spirit (God in us) wants to speak to us. He wants to hear what we have to say. I share my conversations with the Father to demonstrate how much a Great and Holy God desires to have a relationship with His creation. As I searched for years to find intimacy with Christ (God), poems would pour out of my heart. I only recently realized that my Abba, Father, has always heard me, and He has been communicating with me more intimately than I could ever have imagined. I pray that by reading our conversations, you will realize how much our Heavenly Father cherishes our thoughts and words.

I dedicate this book to Jocey, Beth, Bev, Cindy, Diana, Rona, Tina, Mary Jo, and Autumn.

I also want to thank *Theresa*, who has walked with me on this journey of discovering who I am in Christ and embracing His love for me.

Thank you to *Marilyn*, *Nancie, Barbara, Laurie, Nelda, Andrea, Norma and Jane,* my greatest encouragers.

Photo 112645740 @ Giulio Mignani / Dreamstime.com

January

Joy in All We Do

My prayer for the new year is to see a world full of believers who have found the source of joy, and the strength to keep that source close. Joy allows believers to shine God's love in a dark world.

It's easy to mistake happiness for joy, but they are different. Happiness is based on conditions. Joy can **only** come from the Father. Joy is the strength that allows us to worship and praise the Father in all circumstances. One of the most significant examples of joyful praising despite difficult situations is found in Acts 16, specifically in the following verses. Paul and Silas couldn't have been happy with their pain, but their condition could not circumvent their joy!

Acts 16: 22-26 (NLT)

22 A mob quickly formed against Paul and Silas, and the city officials ordered them stripped and beaten with wood rods. 23 They were severely beaten, and then they were thrown into prison. The jailer was ordered to make sure they didn't escape. 24 So the jailer put them into the inner dungeon and clamped their feet in the stocks. 25 Around midnight, Paul and Silas were praying and singing hymns to God, and the other prisoners were listening. 26 Suddenly, there was a massive earthquake, and the prison was shaken.

Habakkuk 3:17-19 (NKJ)

17 Though the fig tree may not blossom, nor fruit be on the vines; though the labor of the olive may fail, and the fields yield no food; though the flock may be cut off from the fold, and there be no herd in the stalls – 18 Yet I will rejoice in *the Lord, I will joy in the God of my salvation. **19** The Lord God is my strength; He will make my feet like deer's feet, and He will make me walk on my high hills.*

The Bible is the word of God,
I've known this since a child.
When the path was arduous that I trod,
I got discouraged and wanted to die.

God brought me back and took my hand,
wrapped me in His arms as He would a child.
His guidance with wisdom I don't understand,
restored me to a state of joy, and a smile.

Meditate a moment if you will,
there's a message in God's book.
His commands back then are pertinent still.
Do you remember? Let's take a look.

In Habakkuk, the picture is bleak.
Possibly even bleaker than today.
No food, no sun, no joy until God speaks,
Great is His Mercy, He has much to say.

"When you remain in Me, I remain in you,
not sometimes but always and forever.
I'm your strength in everything you do.
You can overcome when we are together."

Because of God, my path is set straight.
I run and sing for joy.
I spring into His arms, and I don't hesitate.
His strength fills the void.

The Blessings of a Mother

Children are a reward from our Heavenly Father. I believe it. Today's world doesn't value the life of a child. For years, people would get rid of a child because it was not convenient. We've seen child abuse run rampant, instead of loving them as our Father in Heaven loves us.

I am not naïve enough to think children are easy because they aren't. They take care and require safety and the necessities of life. It doesn't matter if we are not feeling well. When we are too tired to go on, or our finances are low, their needs don't stop. For 18-25 years, we are responsible for growing them and seeing to their education.

I was a single parent to two girls, which made parenting difficult. One evening, my youngest daughter asked me a question that brought the nightmare of divorce home. To explain, I'll share a part of our conversation.

> *"Mommy, I want Daddy. How come Daddy isn't here?"*
>
> *I quickly prayed for guidance from the Holy Spirit for words that would help my four-year-old daughter as she grappled with the harsh reality of divorce.*
>
> *"Honey, your Daddy loves you. I'm sorry he isn't here anymore, but he will come as often as possible. Did you know you have another Daddy, a Heavenly Daddy? God is your Daddy, and He is perfect. He will never leave you, and He will always take care of you."*

After that conversation, I was convinced I could not parent my daughters without help. I asked the Lord if He would partner with me. I know He honored my request because if it weren't for the wisdom of the Holy Spirit, I would not have made it out of their childhood.

My heart grieves for those parents whose children have wandered away from their teachings. I wish I could remove the hurt when children get into trouble or hurt themselves. I think about parents who lose a child and my heart breaks. I pray for special comfort for those parents.

That being said, I will unapologetically thank my God for the blessings of my daughters and His favor on me while I raised them. If you haven't invited the Holy Spirit to give you wisdom in raising your children, it would be wise to consider doing so. Be deliberate and specific about your request. He will not interfere where He isn't invited.

Isaiah 65:23 (NLT)
23 They will not work in vain, and their children will not be doomed to misfortune. For they are people blessed by the Lord, and their children too, will be blessed.

Psalm 127:3-5 (NLT)
3 Children are a gift from the Lord; they are a reward from Him. 4 Children born to a young man are like arrows in a warrior's hands. 5 How joyful is the man whose quiver is full of them! He will not be put to shame when he confronts his accusers at the city gates.

The Father has blessed me all my life.
Blessings so great, I forget about my strife.
But the greatest blessing He has given me
are the most beautiful girls I will ever see.

He gave me daughters to dispel the dark
that always seemed to be a prominent part
of a life lived in chaos and unrest.
Their presence pointed me to my best.

We weathered the challenging days we faced,
and all the time, our Heavenly Father's grace
was there to make sure we never forgot,
through Him, we found the peace we sought.

I'm privileged to have such Godly daughters.
The lives they lived made them stronger.
The loveliness of their souls shines through
in everything they say and do.

My blessings don't end there,
with daughters that care.
Besides the joy they freely impart
I have grandchildren to fill my heart.

Today I'm surrounded by the love of many,
cognizant of those who don't have any.
God's love for my daughters blesses me too,
He has given them husbands who are true.

There are few blessings in this world,
that compares to the truth of God's word,
or the beautiful gift He gives to a mother,
as He cares for her children and others.

Thank you, Lord, for the grace of your gift,
of those around me. Your love never quits.
Remind me every day how blessed I am.
I know whatever I must do, I can!

Blessed Grandparents

I was visiting with a friend earlier today, and our conversation went to ... of course, our children. My friend is in her 70s. She commented on her children and how they sometimes smother her with care. I thought about my own mother. She was an Air Force wife and was forced to be independent and stubborn to keep the family together through the uncertainty of the service.

When Dad died, I was the only child who lived close by. Mom was frail but strong. (Can you be frail and strong?). Still totally independent until the last two months of her life. She lived an hour away, but the girls and I visited as often as we could. Mom's sister lived close by, so she was able help Mom, which relieved me of some of the responsibility.

It was always hard to gauge when I should intervene if I thought she wasn't making a good decision about something, especially health issues. I had to decide if it was something serious enough that I should assert my authority.

I told my friend that when parents get older, the children have difficulty knowing when to allow them their independence and when to insinuate themselves into their care or decisions. There are two extremes, too much interference or not enough.

I then thought about my own children and how difficult it was for me as a parent to know when to allow them their independence or to intervene in their lives. So, at both ends of life, tough decisions must be made.

Today, I am a grandmother of four, two boys and two girls. When my daughters started having children, I had to get used to letting them make the parenting decisions. My daughters clearly stated my responsibility was not to be a parent to their children. They are spiritedly independent and have their own parenting ideas. I had to learn to step back. No matter how much I want to intercede, I don't.

 I still rely on the wisdom of the Holy Spirit to teach me, but now I ask for help to be the best grandmother I can. Society is relegating our older population to extinction because it deems us nonproductive. I say they are wrong! I have created a list of five ways grandparents can make a difference in the family, all beginning with the letter "P." For those who are new to the profession of grandparenting, please allow me to share a few observations.

The foremost important thing I can do is to ***PRAY*** for my grandchildren and their relationship with the Lord. **(1 John 3:1).**

I utilize prayer almost constantly to ask for ***PROTECTION*** from the harshness and heartache of life. In prayer, I petition for God to prevent harm from befalling the grandchildren. I cannot remove all of the bad things that can happen, so when they do, I ask for discernment for ways I can walk alongside the Lord with them through those times to ***PREVENT*** bitterness and anger. **(Psalm 34: 17-18)**

No matter what we do, be it fun or taking care of responsibilities, I ***PRONOUNCE*** the truth of God's word and model how to discern and desire the heart of God. I do this because, as a Grandmother, I am responsible for showing the children how they can ***PRESERVE*** the ideals of a family that lives for and prays to God. **(Psalm 103:17).**

Grandchildren are a reward from God. Take the time to love them and then love them more. **(Proverbs 17:6)**

I John 3:1 (NIV)
1 See what great love the Father has lavished on us, that we should be called children of God and that is what we are! The reason the world does not know us is that it did not know Him.

Psalm 34:17-18 (NIV)
17 The righteous cry out, and the Lord hears them; He delivers them from all their troubles. 18 The Lord is close to the brokenhearted and saves those who are crushed in spirit.

Psalm 103:17-18 (NIV)
17 But from everlasting to everlasting the Lord's love is with those who fear him, and his righteousness with their children's children – 18 with those who keep His covenant and remember to obey His precepts.

Proverbs 17:6 (NIV)
6 Children's children are a crown to the aged, and parents are the pride of their children.

I have two children God gave to me.
There was a time I asked for three,
but my Heavenly Father knew better than I
and said no. Later, I knew why.

I became single when the girls were young.
Turns out two children were better than one.
I was always working to make ends meet.
They played together when I was too beat.

My daughters have children of their own.
Where I fit into their lives has been unknown.
Do I show them wisdom and give advice?
I learned quickly that wasn't my right.

The Bible tells us grandchildren are a reward
given to us so we can love them and adore
without complete responsibility
for the details of raising them into capability.

Grandparents play an essential role,
to assure they grow up healthy and whole.
God told us to pray without ceasing,
invest in them so their wisdom will increase.

Pray for their protection and for their souls,
to come to understand all of those
truths our Heavenly Father declares.
Pray they accept all that is theirs.

As we pray for our grandchildren,
we should also pray for the next generations
that will come from the fruits of our labor
as we point them to lean into God's favor.

My Father's Love

Most of us have learned from birth that God loves us. Cognitively, we have it down without a doubt. One of the first verses we memorize is **John 3:16** – *For god so loved the world He gave His only begotten Son.* The first two songs I remember are "Jesus Loves Me," and "Jesus Loves the Little Children."

What about in our hearts and souls? Can we fathom how wide and deep God's love is for us? Can we believe that the God of the universe loves us dearly? He is the creator of everything. He has always been and always will be. This Great God is in our past, with us now, and is already with us in the future! Yet, He dearly loves each person.

My heart's desire is to be a light in a dark world. I continually come up with brilliant ideas that will make a difference. I excitedly discuss my ideas with God. In my finite mind, I'm just sure He has to think my ideas are amazing ideas, and He can't wait to implement them. It doesn't take long to figure out that my suggestions aren't that great, and I fall flat on my face when I attempt to work them out on my own.

What happens next? I feel foolish and inept and wonder why I even try to do things because, after all, wow, who am I to think I am worth anything? I withdraw back into myself until the next time I hear a sermon about how we are supposed to be a light in a dark world.

This morning, in my early morning musings, I meditated on the mysteries of life. God discussed a correlation between my children and me and me and God, who is My Father.

God told me to remember when my daughters came to me with an idea or a plan or drew a picture that looked like scribbles. How did I react? Did I shame them because their plan didn't make sense? Did I scold them for using up paper to draw junk?

Of course not. I praised them for their ideas and efforts and told them they were the sweetest and greatest of everything. Sometimes I even helped them work on their ideas. My daughters always believed I thought they were geniuses.

So, why would I think a God who loves me more than I love my children and grandchildren would treat me differently? He doesn't. He never will. He loves me. My Heavenly Father cherishes me no matter what I think about, how I feel, or what I do. He willingly came to earth as a human through His Son Jesus, so He could know what it is like to live in humanity. His love is so profound that He gave up His Only Begotten Son so we can be with Him for eternity.

<u>Lamentations 3:21-23 (ESV)</u>
21 But this I call to mind, and therefore I have hope: 22 The steadfast love of the Lord never ceases; His mercies never come to an end; 23 they are new every morning; great is your faithfulness.

<u>I Peter 1:18-19 (ESV)</u>
18 Knowing that you were ransomed from the futile ways inherited from your forefathers, not with perishable things such as silver or gold, 19 but with the precious blood of Christ, like that of a lamb without blemish or spot.

God's perspective is not mine.
He's been the same throughout time.
I went to God and told Him what I could do
to make life better for me and you.

I had such great ideas to impart!
I detailed my idea because I'm so smart.
He would see how fantastic the ideas were.
My ideas came so quickly that they blurred.

Finally, exhausted, I had to stop for a while.
As I closed my eyes, I noticed His smile.
His smile was brilliant and oh, so kind.
He looked at me with His gentle eyes.

I was mesmerized as he held my gaze
and gently took me back through the days
until there was nothing but night.
A place so dark there was no sight.

Puzzled and concerned, I strained my eyes
but still saw nothing. I asked Him why?
What happened to the beauty of the world?
Then I got quiet to wait for His word.

I waited a minute, then another and one more.
While I waited, I searched deep to explore
my knowledge so I could be the one to show
my Father all the amazing things I know.

While I was gathering all of my smarts,
I heard a chuckle that warmed my heart.
Soon the darkness turned to gray,
and I was finally able to see my way.

Then suddenly, through the sunless sky
came a dazzling light; I had to hide my eyes.
A brightness so powerful I fell on my knees
and begged the Father to help me, please.

Right after I cried out, I heard a rumble
that caused me to run, but I stumbled.
I didn't understand what had occurred.
The meaning of it all was obscured.

I had my eyes closed so tight.
My body trembled; I was filled with fright.
I made a point to be very still.
Praying to God that I wasn't ill.

A quiet so dense surrounds me.
Unbidden, my eyes opened, and I could see
just how foolish my finite pride was.
Where I had been caused me to pause.

I was ashamed of my perceived expertise,
but right away, a gentle breeze
surrounded the space I occupied.
I saw the radiance of God's loving smile.

The words I heard Him say to me
were kind and gentle; they set me free.
The message I got so loud and clear
was how much my Father holds me dear.

He told me He loved all of my ideas.
He said they were brilliant and real.
God came to me and took me by the hand
and said – come on, let's make a plan.

Photo 134948060@Maria Rossiitseva / Dreamstime.com

February

Agony to Victory

No one born into this life escapes tragedies. There are different levels of heartbreak, but the emotional fallout is the same despite the circumstances. Hurting, being angry, crying, and looking for answers are all part of the process most of us experience until we get to the other side of grief.

We must not deny our pain when amid our grieving because it will not go away. We can pretend it doesn't affect us for a time, but our emotions will rebel against the suppression.

We can take comfort in having the Holy Spirit with us during the days of mourning. He will not leave us or forsake us in our sorrow. The Comforter will walk with us until we get to the other side of grief.

Despair happens to everyone because of sin and because we live in a fallen world. We are spiritual beings living in a physical body. The real battles we face are not in the flesh but in the spirit. Too often, I try to fight this battle with weapons of the world. It's like fighting cancer with skin lotion or a brain tumor by taking aspirin and lying down. Those kinds of problems demand another type of help. So do spiritual challenges.

The promise of God is that everyone will have despair and be stricken with bad times. We must remain faithful to Him, our Lord, during those times. When we plant His love all around us amid the chaos, we reap a harvest rich with His blessings, and our souls will see laughter.

Jesus already won the war. Praise God for that. He also gave us a doomsday weapon for defeating Satan: the Holy Spirit. Feed the Holy Spirit, and He will nourish our spirit. Proper soul nutrition keeps us alert to the schemes of the enemy.

How do we feed the spirit? By feeding our minds with the Word of God and putting more trust in His truths than your feelings. The chosen received mana daily while wandering in the wilderness. God didn't give them nourishment for a week or month, but every day. Our Good God knows we must nourish ourselves spiritually and physically daily, not once a week or every month.

Psalm 126:5-6 (MSG)
And now, God, do it again – bring rains to our drought-stricken lives so those who planted their crops in despair will shout hurrahs at the harvest, so those who went off with heavy hearts will come home laughing, with armloads of blessing.

Isaiah 35:10 (NLT)
10 Those who have been ransomed by the LORD will return. They will enter Jerusalem singing, crowned with everlasting joy. Sorrow and mourning will disappear, and they will be filled with joy and gladness.

I woke up this morning in a panic
and looked around to identify it.
There is always a reason for my distress.
When I figure it out, my anxiety is less.

My mind went back to yesterday.
As soon as I remembered, I looked for a way
to block the memory I held inside.
The debilitating pain I could not hide.

My body crumpled to the floor.
The despair that came – the grief I wore
blocked out the comfort of the Holy Spirit
so well, I could not feel him a bit.

God! I cried. Father! Savior!
What can explain my behavior?
This agony and wrenching pain
in my life, my God, I cannot retain!

Please take away this cursed despair.
Purge my mind until my memory isn't there.
I don't know how long I lay on the floor.
This is something I've never done before.

The chill of the morning forced me to move,
so the harsh coldness would not be my doom.
Before I got up, I asked myself,
can I escape the dark into which I delved?

I stayed waiting a little longer
until I realized I was stronger.
The coldness of the day, and my cold room,
deadened my pain, and none too soon.

I went to the kitchen and turned on the light.
I see the coffee pot, a source of his delight.
Another wave of agony hit me as I stood.
To live alone, I swore I never would.

The chair close by caught my lifeless body.
I noticed my house shoes were shoddy.
I didn't care but took them both off
and threw them so hard, but I had to scoff.

My house shoes, one at a time, hit the wall,
but the violent action did no damage at all.
Another wave of hysterics flooded my soul.
I sobbed, I screamed, I was out of control.

Hours I spent in agony until the day was over.
I begged God to give me strength before
I melted away into the abyss.
I knew if I did – I wouldn't be missed.

I finally moved from the chair to my room,
plunged into bed, to sleep until noon.
As I drifted into a troubled sleep,
a quiet voice spoke to me so sweet.

The Holy Spirit penetrated my pain
to comfort me and remove my shame.
He said, "You are cherished by Your Father above.
He wraps His arms around you in His love."

I remember His Words, "this too will pass."
He promises me my pain and tears won't last.
So, as I close my swollen grieving eyes,
peace that passes all understanding is inside.

Cry Out to God

We spent many days isolated from the community during the pandemic, which began in 2020. One positive constant during those days was our privilege to share our hearts with God. Amid my agony, words got stuck in my mind, so the Holy Spirit interceded for me.

How do we grieve during a season of life that has us isolated? Might we grieve as David did? He was the King and isolated because he was King. I'm sure his position weighed heavily on him, and he didn't want to show signs of weakness. David trusted God to hear him and never stopped pouring out his heart to the Father.

As a whole, people like to put timelines for unpleasant things. Somehow that gives us a hope that there is an end. Grieving people are no exception. It doesn't matter what limit we "think" two to four, even five years but more realistically, we always feel the loss of our loved ones. On the other side of grief, we can take the strength of our relationship with our loved ones and forge a different life without them.

Cry when you must, don't let anyone tell you when the time to grieve has passed. Laugh when you want, it's okay to smile, laugh, and even be glad of the day because that honors our loved ones as much as letting them know how sorely we miss them. Connect with God often, for God is our comforter and understands our pain even when no one else understands.

Romans 8:26 (ESV)

26 *Likewise the Spirit helps us in our weakness. For we do not know what to pray for as we ought, but the Spirit himself intercedes for us with groanings too deep for words.*

John 14:16 (ESV)

16 And I will ask the Father, and he will give you another Helper, to be with you forever.

Revelation 21:4 (NLT)

4 He will wipe every tear from their eyes, and there will be no more death or sorrow or crying or pain. All these things are gone forever.

God loves His children all the time.
He desires to see us shine.
I questioned Him about these hard days.
I asked Him to help me understand His ways.

These days, God has felt so far away.
I doubt the good, no matter what others say.
God gently reminds me that He is sovereign.
This life we are living is a part of His plan.

He reminds me of those who gave the most.
God's family took time to devote
themselves to others, so they weren't alone.
We gave notes, presents, and calls on the phone.

Stay the course until we meet up yonder.
Romans 12:12* is for us to ponder.
Paul urges us to rejoice in our hope,
which is found in God and helps us cope.

We must be patient in these troubled times
and keep praying for your family, and mine.
Prayers connect our spirits to each other.
Remember the downhearted, help them recover.

Remember, God has no timeline like we do.
He is in the past, present, and future too.
Before creation, He had a plan.
He created the world and made the first man.

God is present with us at the same time.
It's hard to understand in our mind
His goals are set, He knows the outcome.
Everything that happens is to lead us home.

This is the time to hold on to God's truth.
The Holy Spirit is enough proof.
Our acceptance of truth gives us peace,
the kind that everyone seeks.

***Romans 12:12(ESV) – Rejoice in hope, be patient in tribulation, be constant in prayer.**

Why, God?

As a mother, I want to keep my children and grandchildren from trauma. I want to make their lives better than the one I grew up in. I want them to remain forever innocent with no knowledge of how evil can overshadow good things in life.

Unrealistic? Of course, so what's the answer? Recognize what evil CAN do and remember all wisdom and goodness come from our Father. This helps us cohabitate with evil without compromising God's love.

I believe in God's protection. There are over a hundred verses that address His protection. One of my favorites:

Psalm 32:7(NIV) *You are my hiding place; you will protect me from trouble and surround me with songs of deliverance.*

God loves my loved ones and me. He only wants good for us.

BUT WAIT!

What will I believe ... what will I say ... how will I react when a life-changing evil happens to my loved ones? My reaction does not offend God because He is good and loves me. I can go to Him even when I disagree with what He did or did not do.

I learned to rise above my pain when something unpleasant happens to me personally. When my family hurts, a plethora of emotions bombards my soul. The enemy knows this, and he also knows that the surest way to upset my peace is to attack my family, so he does. The enemy is after one thing. To disrupt my peace and contentment in the Father.

Finally, all of the emotions culminate into one volatile emotion called anger. The enemy loves it when I get angry because he can remind me of all the lies he has fed me through the years. Even if I've been delivered from the results of those lies, he can get them to surface when I have pulled away from people and God's protection. There's that word protection again.

I researched God's protection and what it means because we will question God when something disrupts all we believe. Satan would love nothing more than for God's children to be afraid when our world has been rocked, and it appears God did not love us enough to protect our family or us.

Researching didn't give me answers because most articles I found were from someone's perspective on the other side of healing from hurt. Most of my wisdom is seen from the "other side." So, what is the next step? I've asked the Holy Spirit to show me something that made sense, a verse, a passage, or bring anything that can help to my remembrance.

Finally, I heard Him tell me to quit looking and write. I already had the answer I sought, but I wasn't looking for the truth. I was looking for what I wanted the truth to be. Have you ever done that? Look for a specific solution with the outcome that will make the most sense to you. Usually, that answer isn't the truth.

"Okay, Holy Spirit. I'll write, and You talk." He is always kind but firm, gentle but brutally honest. This is the Word I received from my God and Heavenly Father.

"I am the Lord God Almighty, the Great I am. You know that. I provide perfect protection for those who reside under my umbrella. I ask you to get out of your finite body and mind for a short time and try to think like Me. Can you? Of course not. No one can know the mind of God. Start remembering what you know about Me out of the realm of humanity."

God told me that His protection is all about perspective, not only perspective but His perspective. God created man and woman to have a relationship with Him. Still, He wants us to choose that relationship of our free will, not because He commands it or because we are robots and He programmed us to love Him.

The sad reality is that using our free will to venture away from His love did not escape His plan. Because of free will, he chooses not to interfere in our free will, which causes hardships, pain, and hurt. His protection for our Spirit is His ultimate goal so we can be with Him for eternity at the end of days.

God paid a high price for that protection. He asked His only Son to become the perfect sacrificial lamb so that we can be with the Father forever at the time of the death of our physical body. Jesus agreed. When He defeated death and the grave, He ascended back to His Father. Still, He left a comforter for all who have accepted Him as Savior. The Holy Spirit comes into us and will never leave or forsake us. He will never invade our space or insert Himself in our lives without permission.

I don't know why bad things happen to good people or good things happen to bad people, but I don't have to. The bad thing still happened, and the pain is still there. But I know God has already provided me with the perfect protection for all eternity. When I allow God's Spirit to communicate with my spirit, peace is once again restored.

<u>**Romans 8:28 (NLT)**</u>
28 *And we know that God causes everything to work together for the good of those who love God and are called according to his purpose for them.*

.

<u>**Psalm 21:8 (NIV)**</u>
21 You are my hiding place; you will protect me from trouble and surround me with songs of deliverance.

I heard the report and was devastated.
Why did this happen? I don't understand it.
I cried for a while, disappointed and sad,
thinking after this, I can never be glad.

After the sadness was gone, anger welled up
from deep in my soul and wouldn't stop.
I told God of my displeasure.
"Was there a reason for this? Please share."

God allowed me to sit in misery for a time,
until He could pierce the darkness.
After I was utterly, emotionally spent,
I waited for Him to explain His intent.

To my surprise, even though He was kind
He instructed me to go to Job and find
His answers to Job, when he was distressed,
begging God for answers and for some rest.

I read the last chapters when Job asked God
why he had to suffer so, on this path he trod.
He reminded God of his sacrifice and prayer
and about the times he immediately obeyed.

The creator of all heard what Job said.
When Job finished, God said he was misled.
He asked Job who created the world.
God alone has the power to create or destroy.

With each passing word from the Father
Job saw how big God really was.
He realized he had no right to question
a God who was, is and will always be present.

Instead of looking at what we face now,
He wants to hear our praise. I ask Him how?
Praise the Father even if we don't feel it.
This obedience releases the Holy Spirit.

Our Heavenly Father reminded me,
He created us to be with Him and be free.
His plan worked until the enemy came in
and tempted Eve to act out the first sin.

God allows us free will for life.
He brings His creation through all the strife.
Bad things happen because of sin.
That is a fact of life that will be until the end.

One day, Jesus will come for his bride
in a blaze of glory, he will not be denied.
When He does, we will live in a world
of perfection, as He promised in His word.

Lamenting a Hard Life

Life is hard. I've thought that as long as I can remember. It may have to do with the tragedies I experienced as early as eight and the trauma of growing up in a volatile environment. I could give you a list as long as the number of years I've lived of examples of hard – but I won't give it to you now. If you are alive, you've suffered hardships of your own.

I listened to a song, written and performed by **Mercy Me**; *"Even If"*. The words to the chorus spoke to me today:

> *I know You are able, and I know You can save through the fire with Your mighty hand. But even if You don't, my hope is You alone.*

I've heard the song before, but today the Holy Spirit opened my spiritual eyes a bit more and changed my perspective of my life.

As I said, life is hard, but spending time lamenting about it, wishing for a better life, can only breed discontent.

So, what is different from my perspective? I am a bit more confident that I am loved by my Heavenly Father. I've had His **comfort** in the darkest night, His **peace** in the most violent storm, His **compassion** in my greatest pain, and His **love** despite my disillusionment with His provision.

If I had never experienced the hardness of life, I wouldn't know the goodness of my Father. I know what Paul meant when he said he was content in all things, even the hardships because The God of the universe ministered to him.

John 13:7 (NIV)
7 Jesus replied, "You do not realize now what I am doing, but later you will understand."

Romans 5:3-4 (NLT)
3 We can rejoice, too, when we run into problems and trials, for we know that they help us develop endurance 4 And endurance develops strength of character, and character strengthens our confident hope of salvation.

Revelation 21:4 (NIV)
He will wipe every tear from their eyes. There will be no more death or mourning or crying or pain, for the old order of things has passed away.

I spent years lamenting the bad
in my life, and I could never be glad.
I wasted time wishing for a different life,
one with no tragedies, heartache, or strife.

I would cry out to my Heavenly Father.
I asked why good things happened to others.
I begged Him not to continue further.
I didn't see the good, only stormy weather.

I resisted for years, now I understand
how much I've been protected by His hand.
Protection – not as we've been trained
to be protectors of family and friends.

My Father in heaven is the perfect protector.
He guards my spirit and takes my heart
to gently surround it with His perfect love
until the day we will be with Him above.

Contentment is not easily achieved.
We are so enmeshed in what we receive.
If we had more of this and less of that,
our life would be what we expect.

Then the next day comes to us.
What we received doesn't seem like much,
so once again, we make our plans
to get more and be on top once again.

One day while meditating in my spirit
I heard the words: "you just don't get it!"
The thought stopped me in my tracks.
"What are you talking about?" I had to ask.

The Father created the universe
and everything you see on this earth.
He made this world to provide
a special place for His next miraculous act.

His perfect creation was humankind.
He gave His love and never left us behind.
God's enemy had his own version of power.
He schemes to ruin God's world every hour.

Our Heavenly Father always knew
from man's presence He would be removed
because He is holy and cannot tolerate sin.
We disobeyed, and the story begins.

What Satan didn't know
or maybe he did but refused to show
his knowledge and acceptance
of God's plan to lead us to repentance.

For centuries life came and went.
Good and bad continued and wouldn't relent.
But during everyone's life, good and bad,
God gave joy from the sad.

I know now, after all of these years,
our joy is more real because of the tears.
Our victory is here now and complete.
We have no reason to compete.

I want to hold this truth close to my heart
so this new contentment won't part.
I know, however, after trying all of this alone,
that I can never achieve joy on my own.

God also knew this about me
and devised a plan to set me free.
I realize as fully as I can
the priceless act to fulfill His plan.

He gave His Only Begotten Son
so we could again, with Him, be one.
How can I bemoan an imperfect life
and pray God would release me from strife?

When I look at the bigger picture and believe
all of the good God planned for us to receive,
I must thank You, God, Jesus, and Holy Spirit
for working together so we can achieve it.

The wonderous future He planned for us
and even now, as long as we trust,
we have access to his peace and joy.
Amidst the bad is some good, which we enjoy.

Photo 109261575 @ Dero2084 / Dreamstime.com

March

Who Do You Trust?

Do you believe in absolutes? When I was growing up, there were absolutes. We trusted those absolutes. I've seen the world evolve into "better" thinking and more knowledge. We are told there are no absolutes, and everything is relative according to our perceptions. And whatever our perception, it is true to us, which is okay.

How are we supposed to live in unity without absolute truths? I marvel at how people can believe all of this and trust all that we trust but decide that there is no God. I don't know much, but this I know: my God is a God of order, not chaos.

My God is absolute. How can we believe anything we see or hear … when we are constantly told what we experience isn't the truth? The further we stray from God and His truths, the more we believe people have the answers. The more we believe people have the answers, the more people are stepping up to assure us they are the ones with the truth.

Proverbs 3:5-6 (NIV)
5 Trust the Lord with all your heart and lean not on your own understanding; 6 in all your ways submit to Him, and He will make your paths straight.

Philippians 4:6-7 (ESV)
6 Do not be anxious about anything, but in everything by prayer and supplication with thanksgiving, let your requests be made known to God. 7 And the peace of God, which surpasses all understanding, will guard your hearts and your minds in Christ Jesus.

Psalm 118:8 (NIV)
It is better to take refuge in the Lord than to trust in man.

Our Father who art in heaven,
Your love has given us a safe haven.
I beg – no, I don't beg. I don't have to.
I know you make everything new.

All you ask of me is to step back and see
how You work to set the captive free.
The enemy wants nothing more than to rob us
of the peace that comes from trust.

God, we trust only because of You.
It's all about what we've already seen you do.
The miracles You give us every day
Leave us speechless, with nothing to say.

My Father God, in Jesus' name
I will step back and see once again
the width, the depth, and the height
as your brilliance forges a path in the night.

I have no doubt that You love me.
Please, Lord, help my unbelief.
You alone are worthy of being praised,
You alone – my dark countenance can raise.

Show me You – and show me the way.
I want to hear only the truth. You say
nothing in this world can hurt us
because, in You, we put our trust.

Thank you, my God, My Savior, my King.
Let Your joy fill me so I can sing
of the wonderous love You generously give,
so, we in Your joy and protection can live.

Thank You, my God, my Savior, my King!
Let Your joy fill me so I can sing
the wondrous love You give.
Remind us, in Your protection, we live!

Who Gives You Your Thoughts?

The Pharisees had distorted thinking. They couldn't see past their own pious philosophy. In their opinion, what Jesus said or did was an affront to God.

I wonder how many blessings I have overlooked because of the filter I have in place. I pray to accept God's truth immediately instead of filtering it through the enemy's distortion. "Dear Father in Heaven, I receive the peace You have deposited inside of me."

In **John 6: 5-7,** Jesus asked Philip what they would feed the crowds, not because He didn't have the answer. He already had a plan. He asked Philip as a test to determine his faith.

Jesus does the same thing today. If my money ran out before the end of the month, my Father already knew about it and had a plan to take care of my needs.

There are different choices I could make on how I react. I could become anxious and frantically look for a solution, or I could decide not to give in to fear because I have faith God has it under control. Even then, I might formulate a logical solution to remedy the situation on my own.

The option that pleases the Father is to give it entirely over to Him to resolve without my ideas. His solution is by far better than anything I could devise.

John 6: 5-7 (NLT)

5 Jesus soon saw a huge crowd of people coming to look for him. Turning to Philip, he asked, "Where can we buy bread to feed all of these people?" 6 He was testing Philip, for he *already knew what he was going to do. **7.** Philip replied, "Even if we worked for months, we wouldn't have enough money to feed them."*

<u>Philippians 4:6-7 (NIV)</u>
***6** Do not be anxious about anything, but in every situation, by prayer and petition, with thanksgiving, present your requests to God. **7** And the peace of God, which transcends all understanding, will guard your hearts and your minds in Christ Jesus.*

I asked my Father a question today.
"How will I make it until I get paid?"
He knew what was in my checking account
and what money was scheduled to come out.

I looked at my account and cleared my mind.
I needed this fixed before I was out of time.
I know God loves me, and I know He cares.
God will never forsake me is easy to share.

It isn't so easy to take truth into my heart.
I've never done it, but I want to start.
So, this time I vowed I would remain calm
and remember from where my help comes.

Even though I still had peace inside,
I couldn't get my thoughts to subside.
I can ask to have my car payment deferred.
This was something I had used before.

I talked with the account administrator,
he gave me a plan which was much greater
than anything I could imagine myself.
God told me to put my ideas on the shelf.

His goodness did not stop there.
I went home praising Him in prayer.
I looked at my bank account to make sure
another shortfall didn't occur.

What I saw caused me to blink.
I saw something there I could never think.
In my account, a sizable deposit was made
from a request I made that was delayed.

I made the request two years ago
and decided back then it just wasn't to be so.
For once, I did not worry and fret
about something that hadn't happened yet.

At the perfect time when I needed it most,
a gift came from God, more than I hoped.
Thank you, Father, for your patience with me
until your goodness I could see.

Whose Voice Do You Hear?

We live in a fallen world. There remain conflicting voices in our heads until we exchange our decaying bodies for the promised new ones. The two voices are pulling us either toward victory or defeat. Both voices will appear to be sound advice unless we are prayed up.

Jesus tells us in John that we, His sheep, recognize the Good Shepherd's voice. When I find myself in my head in a debate, the first question I must ask is which voice is God's truth. If the message I hear causes angst, it isn't the Father. If the voice I hear suggests something that will cause chaos, it isn't the Father's. God is a God of order, and his way is the way to peace, not turmoil.

We must beware, however, because the Holy Spirit may be taking us into a complicated place, and the enemy is urging us to take the easy path. Easy is not necessarily of the Lord.

The ideal tool for all children of God is to become so acquainted with our Father's voice as He communes with us that we don't have to think about choosing. The more I read the Word and listen to the Holy Spirit, the more confidence I have in discerning what is from my Heavenly Father and what is from my fleshly father (Satan). Staying in the Word and allowing my spirit to connect to Holy Spirit gives me confidence that I am listening to the Father.

Romans 8:14 –15 (NIV)

14 For those who are led by the Spirit of God are the children of God. 15 The Spirit you received does not make you slaves, so that you live in fear again; instead, the Spirit you received brought about your adoption to sonship. And by him we cry, Abba, Father.

John 6:63 (ESV)
63 It is the Spirit who gives life; the flesh is no help at all. The words that I have spoken to you are Spirit and life.

John 14:26 (ESV)
26 But the Helper, the Holy Spirit, whom the Father will send in my name, He will teach you all things and bring to your remembrance all that I have said to you.

Psalm 85:8 (ESV)
8 Let me hear what God the Lord will speak, for He will speak peace to His people, to His saints; but let them not turn back to folly.

I heard the lies of Satan from the first day.
I knew his voice, so I heard what he said.
There's another voice I want to hear instead.
I hear both causing my healing to be delayed.

Even after years my success never came.
In despair, I tried to find something to blame.
Sometimes people gave me a temporary high,
but then a reality set in that I could not deny.

I woke up to a dark and cloudy world.
I forced myself up, hoping for good to unfurl.
Contradictory thoughts in my head swirled,
causing confusion and distortion to churn.

How long will I wait to take a stand
against an enemy that doesn't understand
his imminent demise is planned?
His destruction will be by God's own hand.

Beginning today, I want to decide
that I will no longer look for a free ride.
I will no longer cower from life or hide.
I will listen to God and stay by His side.

Going forward, I won't live in defeat
or turn from the battle in retreat.
I will stand firmly planted on my feet
and experience God's sweet victory.

How to Know the Mind of Christ

Jesus wants to spend time with me. He also wants me to know and understand who I am and why He created me. The more I understand myself, as seen in His eyes, the more I want to spend time with Him. I must get to know Him because He is in me, and I am in Him. I can only do the will of the Father if I know what it is. Unless I spend time with Him, I won't ever get to know Him, and I won't know what His will is.

Why is it hard for me to want to be around and know people? Because I have a hard time with intimacy. That's the stronghold. I don't want to open up and be intimate. I don't mind being vulnerable, but intimacy, not so much. So, I keep coming against this brick wall that never crumbles. My hugs are sincere but never engaging. No, it isn't all or nothing. I want to allow this door to be unlocked and all the lies purged so I can know how deep God's love is.

Psalm 139:1-4 (NIV)
1 You have searched me, Lord, and you know me. 2 You know when I sit and when I rise; you perceive my thoughts from afar. 3 You discern my going out and my lying down; you are familiar with all my ways 4 Before a word is on my tongue you, Lord, know it completely.

James 4:8 (NLT)
8 Come close to God, and God will come close to you. Wash your hands, you sinners; purify your hearts, for your loyalty is divided between God and the world.

I stand at the entrance and stare.
Inside are people; I wish I wasn't here.
I step into the room shrouded in fog.
I know immediately, I don't belong.

My presence in the room is surreal.
I stand and wish I could let go and feel
the camaraderie of everyone inside.
Instead, I look for somewhere to hide.

I see an empty chair alone in a corner.
I move towards the safety, I'm the owner.
The chair was definitely put there for me.
It's a perfect place to be and allows me to see.

I'm content sitting there listening to others
carry on conversations. No one bothers
to approach me to find out who I am.
The comfort of not being seen is my plan.

I look at my watch, ready to go,
thinking if I left, would anyone know?
As I sat and wondered when I could leave,
something happened I would never believe.

I lost the safety of my anonymity
when I realized this person had noticed me.
He reached for my hand and pulled me up.
I was compelled to go; I could not stop.

He walked me into a room glittering in light.
We stopped so I could take in the sight.
I saw everyone there as clearly as day
and everyone saw me, to my dismay.

I could no longer pretend they couldn't see
this person, who turned out to be me.
I dropped the hand of the stranger there.
I wanted to run; I didn't care.

I started back to the room with the clouds
where voices were muffled and not loud.
A gentle touch on my arm held me back.
I searched His face for the courage I lacked.

Soon we were surrounded everywhere
and I knew there wasn't anything to fear.
No one spoke a word right then,
but all eyes turned toward my friend.

They waited to hear what He might say,
I had a desire to remain, so I stayed.
I noticed His eyes as He looked at me.
I knew that deep into my soul, He could see.

Then He started speaking
sweet words as he gently
put His arms around me.
I have never felt such peace.

He spoke; "Everyone, let me introduce you
to someone unique and beautiful who
touches all she meets with kindness
and dispels the dark with her brightness.

I'm so very proud of this daughter of mine
She has loved me from the beginning of time.
It doesn't matter how difficult her life
or the devastating trauma or strife.

She has a pure soul despite it all.
I want to tell you how much she's evolved
into a woman who has captured my heart
and my love for her will never depart.

Please surround this precious one,
whom I cherish as much as I do my Son,
with your friendship and love you reserve
for only the special ones who deserve.

I give her the highest praise and appreciation.
So show her how much she has become
A cherished one of the Most- High King
Which is by far the most important thing."

Photo 77815919 @ Sherah Martin / Dreamstime.com

April

God Is Still God

I cannot remember a time such as this. Maybe you have heard reports that this pandemic, now going into its third year, is from God. My answer to that is, of course, it is. God is sovereign, all-mighty, and the universe is at His disposal because ... oh, yes, it is His creation. He doesn't cause hardships; sin does that. He is always in control. Things can get just as good as they are terrible in a blink of an eye. Will He choose to do that? I don't know, but He does have a word for us until He unfolds His design.

I encourage you to read the entire chapter of Psalm 19 and pray you can find as much encouragement as I did. A word of warning, the enemy will do all he can to make you think you are too weary. I quite often use that excuse. The truth, though, is from where does our strength come? You are correct; it comes from God.

The last time I checked, God is still God, and He has not relinquished His throne, which means we are His children under His umbrella of love. Take courage in God's strength and let His light shine in a dark world!

John 1:3 (ESV)
1 All things were made through him, and without him was not anything made that was made.

Isaiah 44:6 (ESV)
6 Thus says the Lord, the King of Israel and his Redeemer, the Lord of hosts: "I am the first and I am the last; besides me there is no god."

17 Ah, Lord God! It is you who have made the heavens and the earth by your great power and by your outstretched arm! Nothing is too hard for you.

I saw my Bible sitting on the shelf.
"Oh, there it is!" I said to myself.
I looked at the time and considered my day.
Do I have time to hear what God might say?

A little voice told me to read and benefit.
Get up, open the book and just do it.
The Lord led me to **Psalm nineteen**.
I read the first and last verses and in between.

With a single word, God gave us the sun,
and it will stay there until our time is done.
Is there anything that produces more light?
Can anyone else rescue us from our plight?

I look at verse seven and gaze into the sky.
His instructions are clear; my soul is revived.
Verse eight goes on without a wrinkle,
only God can make the complicated simple.

If I pay attention, my soul is filled with light,
because His Word is always good and right.
When I hear His voice and do my part,
His strength penetrates joy into my heart.

There isn't anything as clean and pure
as our Lord's love for us; of this, I'm sure.
So – during these days of isolation,
look to the true comforter for consolation.

His precepts are more precious than gold,
His great love for us is solid and bold.
The strength to get you through today
is to listen and hear what our God has to say.

Our Unknowable God

Through the years, man has searched for knowledge to be better, go farther, and know more than anyone in the universe. In other words, man has been seeking to BE God. Why is that? Go back to Genesis. The search for power to be like God began with Lucifer or Satan. God threw Lucifer out of heaven along with his followers because they desired to be greater than God.

Fast forward to the Garden of Eden. God created Adam and Eve and gave them a home in the garden. Satan, in the form of a serpent, went to Eve and found a way to wake up the sin of pride. But because of a love we can never understand, our creator didn't let the story end there.

<u>**Genesis 3:1-5 (NLT)**</u>
1 The serpent was the shrewdest of all the wild animals the LORD God had made. One day he asked the woman, "Did God really say you must not eat the fruit from any of the trees in the garden?" 2 "Of course we may eat fruit from the trees in the garden," the woman replied. 3 "It's only the fruit from the tree in the middle of the garden that we are not allowed to eat. God said, 'You must not eat it or even touch it; if you do, you will die'." 4 "You won't die!" the serpent replied to the woman. 5 "God knows that your eyes will be opened as soon as you eat it, and you will be like God, knowing both good and evil."

<u>**John 3:16 NLT**</u>

16 For this is how God Loved the world: He gave His one and only Son so that everyone who believes in Him will not perish but have eternal life.

This morning while I walked,
I didn't choose to talk.
Today I wanted to listen
to God speak without hesitation.

I know my God speaks
differently than we seek.
But His message is always true
for me and for you too.

The temperature was perfect.
I left the house ready to connect
with the birds and dogs and cats,
to hear words that would last.

The streets and yards were wet
from the residual rain and yet
I know the dampness is evidence
of a good God's benevolence.

I felt the complexities of the universe.
It's taken people centuries to diligently search
for answers to what keeps the sun in the sky.
The stars only shine at night; why?

For centuries, the human race
has attempted to duplicate and replace
God's handiwork, never acknowledging how
we have intelligence, which God endowed.

I understand how easy it is
to do life ourselves, which gives
us the illusion we are self-sufficient.
Science tells us we are magnificent.

I shudder to think about the time
when Jesus comes back to us and finds
a population of egotistical beings
who take credit for everything.

As He did with a swoop done in fury,
God will erase centuries of theory.
He will finally take His people home,
where we will worship Him on His throne.

Those who don't acknowledged his majesty,
who mocked Him and created this fantasy
will understand then what a mistake
they made, but then it will be too late.

Understanding the Trinity

God – The Father
God – The Son
God – The Holy Spirit

There are three persons under one majestic God of the universe, and each person has specific responsibilities. All three have the same characteristics because they are God. The finite human mind cannot conceive that kind of a being, so we must break it down into different entities in order to take in the Trinity. To do that, we view each one separately: God, Jesus, Holy Spirit. Of the three, the Holy Spirit is the least known and understood by the general Christian Community. But that is a conversation for another time.

I had the Trinity so segregated that I focused on Jesus, the Son. He had the qualities that allowed me to embrace goodness and gentleness. God, the Father, was the disciplinarian and did not have a nurturing quality. Because of my experience with authority, I was afraid of Him, not in awe of Him. I was never able to think about approaching God the Father, ever.

After years of working through the lies of the enemy and the deceit of my memories, I gradually became intrigued by a good Father. I decided to take a step towards getting to know Him. It's been an exciting journey.

Isaiah 64:8 (KJV)

8 But now O Lord, thou art our Father; we are the clay, and thou our potter; and we all are the work of thy hand.

<u>**Psalm 68:5**</u> **(KJV)**
5 A father of the fatherless, and a judge of the widows, is God in his holy habitation.

<u>**Matthew 23:9**</u> **(KJV)**
9 And call no man your Father upon the earth: for one is your Father, which is in heaven.

Jesus and I went for a walk one day.
This wasn't right, did He forget the way?
We've never been this way before.
Did He change paths because He was bored?

Before I could verbalize my question to Him,
we could go no further; the path came to an end.
Surprise was written all over my face.
"Why did we end up here in this place?"

I looked at Him, and He looked at me.
His gaze was so intense I knew He could see
the questions I had and all of my fears,
the intense feelings I've hidden for years.

His soothing tender voice spoke to my heart.
He had a message He wanted to impart.
He said "You have traveled far in your life,
and looked for answers to end all the strife.

"There is one thing you've never tried before.
You got close but never opened the door.
Let me introduce you to someone who cares,
someone who has loved you all these years.

"From the beginning He wants you to know
if you run to Him, He knows where to go.
You've read His book and His instructions,
but you decided there was a better direction.

"We stopped because your eyes saw an end.
But the truth is, this is where you begin.
This path was created for you alone.
It is the one that will take you home.

"Open your eyes and fix your gaze high.
Look beyond the clouds into the sky.
See – Waving to you is God the Father,
He's asking you to go just a bit farther."

I saw God, through my unbelieving eyes.
The sight convinced me my fears were lies.
This person I see doesn't look harsh at all!
He isn't aloof or distant; I can hear His call.

The words I hear and what He speaks
penetrate my heart; they are so sweet.
I look back at Jesus and ask, "what's next?
Please show me the next step."

I saw His eyes sparkle with humor and love.
Good-naturedly, He gave me a shove.
"I don't have to tell you where to go.
Inside of you is information you know.

"The next phase of your life's journey
is a path the Father meant for you only.
The Father knows the way you like to travel.
He made the way easy since you're fragile."

Jesus can always uniquely surprise me.
When I get lazy He reminds me to see
there's more out there that I must learn.
He has given me all the tools so I can discern.

My gaze changes and I see Father, God.
There's a yearning in my heart I find odd.
With only one step toward my Father
I realize there's no need to go any farther.

The minute I took one step alone,
the Father embraced me and loved me home.
He whispered a sweet message in my ear,
"Welcome home. I'm glad you are here."

Our Good, Good, God

There is a worship song called "Goodness of God" from Bethel Music. I won't give you the entire piece, but I encourage you to look it up for all the words. The words that mean the most are in the bridge: *"Your goodness is running after me,"* followed by the first line of the chorus: *"All my life You have been faithful."*

HOW AWESOME is this to know that God pursued us even before we knew there was a God. I ponder these words and realize that I only have a relationship with the Lord because He chose me first.

The God of the universe wants to love, cherish and be in conversation with me.

Romans 8:28 (NASB)

28 And we know that God causes all things to work together for good to those who love God, to those who are called according to His purpose.

James 1:17 (NIV)

17 Every good and perfect gift is from above, coming down from the Father of the heavenly lights, who does not change like shifting shadows.

My God, My Savior, My Jesus, My Lord!
How beautiful is the sum of all Your Words!
You gave me your Holy Spirit from above
to fill my soul with Your love.

You came to me when I was a child
and stayed even when the ride was wild.
You pursued me every time I strayed
and rejoiced when I stopped and waited.

Before long, I deviated again.
You pursued me until I stopped, and then
when You touched my right hand with Yours
I knew immediately I was secure.

Dear God, my Abba Father, out of the many,
You chose me to help others see
how to maneuver through this life
with You, where they'll experience Your delight.

Photo 98645098 @ Darrell Young / Dreamstime.com

May

Is Judgment Coming?

We talk about the love of God often. We should because God is Love, but also Truth and Righteousness. The Old Testament is as relevant today as it was when it was written because our Heavenly Father is the same yesterday, today, and tomorrow.

There comes a time when we must consider the judgment of God. He does not make it a secret that we will be judged eventually. Jeremiah warns the people about the state of affairs in Jerusalem and pronounces God's coming judgment. The children of Benjamin were told to flee from Jerusalem so they would escape the great destruction.

These days the state of affairs is not much different than in Jeremiah's day. God is patient, but there will come a time when He will no longer allow the world to go on the way it is. Soon, God, the Father, will tell Jesus Christ it is time for Him to collect His bride. On that day, we will have to face judgment.

John 3:20-21 (NLT)
20 All who do evil hate the light and refuse to go near it for fear their sins will be exposed. 21 But those who do what is right come to the light so others can see that they are doing what God wants.

John 12:31 (NLT)
31 The time for judging this world has come, when Satan, the ruler of this world, will be cast out.

This morning Lord, I came to You.
I read Jeremiah 6, and now I'm blue.
You gave him warnings and words
of coming destruction with the sword.

You listed their offenses and acts of hate.
You warned them, and now you can't wait
to bring judgment because of their pride
and their refusal to in You abide.

The list of transgressions are many.
You looked for the faithful, there weren't any.
Jeremiah spoke of violence in the streets
and groups of malcontents meeting together.

The objective of their plan
was to rebel against your design.
Their rebellion was complete
because they thought they could compete.

Lord, how arrogant was Jerusalem.
They took what they wanted on a whim
with no regard for the homeless or children
crying for someone to be concerned.

Right became wrong, and evil was right.
They hid in the day and came out at night.
Their intent was to completely control
the entire city while the good was not bold.

You searched the city far and wide
for even one person remaining on your side.
You promised if you could find one
Your judgment of destruction wouldn't come.

Alas - after much effort, you finally gave up.
You raised enemies who would usurp
a people once blessed by your hand
with goodness and wealth across the land.

Why should the past make me blue?
Because You are Holy through and through,
yesterday, tomorrow, and today,
and you still demand that people to live your way.

America is a nation of people that once was
loyal to honor Your precepts and laws.
We took care of the hurting and the sad.
We honored the good and punished the bad.

These honorable actions didn't look right.
They honored the dark and rejected the light.
I read about your judgment in the past
and realized our prosperity won't last.

We see violence in the streets.
The rebellious get together and meet
to plan and take what you meant for good
to destroy and do nothing they should.

The reality of America today
causes me to shudder and try to find a way
to sound the alarm and warn the passive
to take a stand against the evil masses.

I want to cry out a warning
of pending heresy and destruction.
Our way of life is going to see
an end when we are no longer free.

In despair, Lord, I come to you.
Please tell me what I can do.
I see the future and become afraid
because we're destroying all You made.

The sweet words of my Father came.
He comforted me, saying He is the same
as He has always since the beginning been.
He reminded me when all is done, we win.

In my Spirit, God showed me His power
so great that He will never let even one hour
pass when He allows any changes to the plan
He has had since before time began.

Holy Spirit reminded me what
Jesus accomplished on the cross.
His sacrifice was the ultimate way
to allow us to commune with Him every day.

The Father told me it wasn't my task.
To make others good is not what He asks.
His desire and His plan are always for me
to love and praise him and know I'm free.

He chose me to be adopted into
His family of those who remain true
to the creator of the universe.
He alone controls the future of the curse.

God my Father, Jesus Christ, and Holy Spirit
are in control, and I won't ever again doubt it.
One day He will decide, and it won't be long,
to take His family to our everlasting home.

Is Judgment Here?

Destructive hurricanes. Global pandemic. Wars and rumors of wars. Attacks by terrorists from many countries. Deadly earthquakes. Out-of-control fires threaten to destroy an entire state. Groups of God's servants and their families are martyred. The anguished overriding question from the people of the world is, "If there is a God, where is He?"

I cried these words when I was molested as a young child. I heard this cry when my baby brother died; we didn't have enough to eat, and my baby sister took her own life. I heard this cry when my marriage ended, and my children were hurting, whenever I saw an unexplained horror. My cry is internal because my spirit knows precisely where God is.

Whenever I cry out those words, my spirit answers, "God is where He has always been and always will be." The only constant we have is knowing where God is. So, why do bad things happen to good people? Why do bad things happen at all? Because God created us with a mind, the ability to observe and learn, but most importantly, He gives us a free choice which leaves an opportunity for people to do bad things. Nature was designed for enjoyment, but God gave us conditions and rules to follow so nature could take care of us. In our greed, we choose to ignore the laws of the universe.

God has the power and ability to intercede in the world. I can never understand when or how He makes the decision to intervene. Still I know without a doubt that God is the only source we can trust without hesitation. Many, even among believers and sometimes especially believers, wonder why a good and loving God can allow such horrors. If He is as powerful as believers say, why does He not choose to intercede all the time?

God is the author of the universe, world, and time. At the beginning of the world's existence, God had a plan. His goals and purposes have always been to have a perfect relationship with his creation, the kind Adam and Eve experienced before the fall. **(Genesis Chapter 1).** We don't know how long they were in communion with God before Satan interfered with their tranquility. We have free will, so we can choose to stray away from our path because we decide, as our children sometimes do, that the rules are too restrictive.

God is perfectly righteous and cannot relate to imperfection. Not because He does not love us, but because He is too righteous and holy. Think about a genius with a high IQ. They cannot understand why I struggle with a simple formula in algebra. They did algebra at the age of five. Most of the time, geniuses do not associate with someone who cannot communicate with them.

The difference between a genius and God is His desire to communicate with us. He wanted to understand what we experience, so He chose to become man Himself (in the name of Jesus Christ), allowing Himself to know how we experience life.

I am no great philosopher or a brilliant theologian, but I have life experiences. I am convinced that no matter what bad happens to me, God knew about it before time. He had already worked out a way for it to help me in life. God is omnipotent (all powerful), omniscient (knows everything, always), and omnipresent (is everywhere at the same time). He will say when enough is enough. After we accept Jesus as our Savior and are baptized with the Holy Spirit, we have Him with us always … in the good and bad times.

God is loving, and He forgives and intercedes for us. He does not remove consequences when we go against His structure. So, global warming is not what God is doing to our planet, and death and destruction are not because God hates us and creates bad things to punish us. We are responsible for the destruction because of how we choose to live.

God is the author of life from the time of creation, but unlike most novels, He also gives us the ending.

Revelation 21:4 (AB)
4 And He will wipe away every tear from their eyes; and there will no longer be death; there will no longer be sorrow and anguish, or crying, or pain; for the former order of things has passed away.

Romans 5:3-4 (NLT)
3 We can rejoice, too, when we run into problems and trials, for we know that they help us develop endurance. 4 And endurance develops strength of character, and character strengthens our confident hope of salvation.

Romans 8:28 (ESV).
8 And we know that for those who love God all things work together for good, for those who are called according to His purpose.

I said to God the other day,
can you tell me what is going on?
I listened to what He had to say,
it didn't take Him long.

"Of course, I can tell you if I want.
I don't know what good it will do.
You seem to want to flaunt
your independence and call Me a fool.

I've waited for you for many years
to get your act together,
but in return, I receive sneers
and insistence you can do better.

I long for the days before Adam and Eve's sin
when I directly communed with them.
Together we walked in harmony then.
Then they rebelled, and away they ran.

I chose a group of people again.
I gave provisions and guidance to them.
They didn't understand the love I had
was only to make them glad.

Alas, that plan did not succeed,
but I was not surprised.
As your creator, I know what you seek.
The laws I gave for protection were despised.

My chosen people has a tumultuous history
with many ups and downs.
My approval remained a mystery.
I put my plan in place to send my only Son.

The world was dark with angry voices
when Jesus made His entrance.
He showed love and taught good choices.
He promoted true repentance.

My ultimate gift was Calvary's cross.
No words can describe how difficult it was.
I paid for your freedom no matter the cost.
We know our sacrifice was for a great cause.

Right now, we are years from Calvary.
My plan is the same and in the final stages.
I've allowed this pandemic you see
to spotlight what's going on in the nation.

You have gotten so complacent and satisfied.
You don't seek My love or My wisdom.
You listen to friends, thinking they are wise.
Your wisest man is met with my criticism.

I was forced to get the attention of everyone,
significant enough for the world to pause.
I want my flock to admit what they've done.
I want you to discover the root cause.

I've warned you as much as I can do.
I made time for you to forget your busyness,
to search my Word and get back to the truth.
It's time to repent and stop destructiveness."

God's Perfect Plan
John 18 & 19

Two things I picked up on which I've never realized before. The first time Jesus asked who they sought; the soldiers answered. Jesus admitted, "I am He." They fell back and down when He spoke because Jesus' divinity and power were evident. It was God's subtle way of declaring that no number of soldiers could stand against an all-powerful God unless He chose to allow it. Jesus had control of the situation the entire time.

The second was the "other" disciple. I researched to find out who that disciple was. The most popular consensus, though not proven, is that it was John, the disciple Jesus loved. The one factor that refutes it was John is that this disciple was recognized in the Chief Priest's circle and was allowed in. Some say that the servant recognized John because he sold fish. Still, others say they didn't think John could have been known, so it had to have been another follower such as Nicodemus, who was privy to the inner circle.

I noticed that Pilate asserted to the crowds three times that he found no fault with Jesus. The exact number of times Peter denied Jesus. One of Jesus' faithful followers who had been with Him during his three years of ministry denied his association. One person who had only heard about things and didn't know Jesus from Adam was convinced Jesus had done no wrong.

John 18:4-6 (ESV)
4 The Jesus, knowing all that would happen to Him, came forward and said to them, "Whom do you seek?" 5 They

answered Him, "Jesus of Nazareth." Jesus said to them, "I am He." Judas who betrayed Him, was standing with them. 6. When Jesus said to them, "am He," they drew back and fell to the ground.

John 18:15-16 (ESV)
15 Simon Peter followed Jesus, and so did another disciple. Since that disciple was known to the high priest, he entered with Jesus into the courtyard of the high priest, 16 But Peter stood outside at the door. So the other disciple, who was known to the high priest, went out and spoke to the servant girl who kept watch at the door, and brought Peter in.

John 18:38 (NLT)
38 "What is truth?" Pilate asked. Then he went out again to the people and told them, "He is not guilty of any crime."

John 19: 4 & 6 (NLT)
4 Pilate went outside again and said to the people, "I am going to bring Him out to you now but understand clearly that I find Him not guilty." 6 When they sawn Him, the leading priests and temple guards began shouting "Crucify Him! Crucify Him!" Take Him yourselves and crucify Him," Pilate said, "I find Him not guilty."

A contingent of soldiers showed up that night
to confront one man who showed no fright.
Jesus answered, "I am He." Those three words
He spoke, and His divinity was observed.

Jesus spoke with so much power
they fell back and down and cowered.
His love for us was so great
our Savior did not react with hate.

The soldiers once again stood tall,
and Jesus, once more, asked who they sought.
This time they showed a little more bravery,
when Jesus revealed His identity.

All 500 soldiers rushed in
and bound this man who knew no sin.
Then in an impulsive Peter-like act,
he ran forward and used his sword to attack.

Jesus showed His divinity and love.
He healed the soldier and kept him calm.
Instead of allowing one more act of violence,
He let the men and Judas pounce.

The amazing love of our Lord
is so evident throughout His word.
But when the time of His sacrifice came
with love, He willingly endured the pain.

Jesus proved his identity of being God's Son
because from the beginning until it was done,
He fulfilled His mission but kept His power.
He remained in control every hour.

Jesus' life and His death demonstrated
His love when He never hesitated
to willingly give Himself over to them.
10,000 angels were ready to rescue Him.

Thank You, Heavenly Father, for Your love,
that You sent Your only son from above
to pay the price in death for our sin.
You showed Your power when He rose again.

You didn't end there because You knew
as long as we are here, no matter what we do,
we have no strength, not one bit
without your filling of the Holy Spirit.

Dear Lord and Father, Holy Spirit, and God,
We pray for strength to continue to trod
through the time here that You have given to us
to show Your grace as You teach us to trust.

It Isn't About My Ability

If twelve believers are sitting at a table and a facilitator asks these two questions:

1) Is God capable of doing anything He wants when He wants?
2) If you answered yes, why?

I will assume that everyone answered yes to the first question, so that leaves us to consider the second question, "why?"

Some possible answers:

1) Because He is God,
2) God created the world and everything in it, so He can change whatever He wants,
3) God is master of the universe and everything in it.

I could go on with different variations stating the same thing.

I agree with the above answers, so my following questions may surprise some because it isn't something we go to often.

Why do we think that we can do anything for the Lord that He cannot do Himself? Why do we strive to have more faith, thinking if we do, God will be able to perform more miracles or take care of the world better? Why do we think it's up to us to volunteer at every opportunity so that we can work for the Lord and do His work here on earth?

I was in a small group recently, and we did a study on John. On a particular day, **John 11** was our focus. The Lord took my thoughts about faith down a different path than I usually follow. I have often been told that we can do anything if we have enough faith. Or if we prayed for something that didn't happen, the answer is to let us know if we would have had more confidence, our prayers would have been answered the way we asked. (God always answers prayers). I have spent hours agonizing over my lack of faith. Faith is not as clear-cut as we like to think. Consider Martha's faith. **(John 11:21-27).** She took the position, "Jesus can do anything He wants *if He decides to do it.* But He doesn't always decide to do what we ask for."

Martha struggled with her faith versus the logic of the situation. We know her faith was strong because she reiterated to Him that she had always believed that He was the Messiah. She believed He would heal if He decided to, but He didn't, so Lazarus died.

Martha indicated that she believed Jesus could do something for Lazarus even after death. Still, when Jesus took steps to do the very thing she knew He could do, she protested because, logically, the smell of death would be overwhelming.

The revelation from Holy Spirit is that Jesus does not need our unfailing faith for Him to do good things for us. We can waiver in our faith, but His work still goes on. I am comforted by that fact. Nothing is about me. It is all about Jesus, God, and the Holy Spirit and how they work together for the good of those who belong to the Father.

The beautiful realization is my Father loves me just because He loves me, not because of what I can do for Him or even how good I am. I will never live up to His standards without the blood, and He doesn't need me to do anything for Him since He has all and is all. I thank the Lord for His magnanimously unfailing love.

<u>**John 11:21 – 22 (NLT)**</u>
21 Martha said to Jesus, "Lord if only you had been here, my brother would not have died. 22 But even now, I know that God will give you whatever you ask".
<u>**John 11:27 (NLT)**</u>
27 Yes, Lord," she told him. "I have always believed you are the Messiah, the Son of God, the one who has come into the world from God".

I had a conversation with my God today.
But I didn't know what to say.
I had prayed with as much faith as possible
about a situation for which I felt responsible.

The perfect solution was at hand,
so I prayed and vowed to take a stand.
I guess my faith just wasn't enough
because it didn't work out and I felt rebuffed.

I asked My Heavenly Father what I had to do
to increase my faith and my trust too.
I didn't get a word from God when I asked,
so, I, not so patiently, waited as time passed.

I was just about to leave; I didn't want to wait.
I was meeting a friend and I was late.
As I stood up, I heard a gentle voice.
I froze right there; I had no choice.

the words were kind, so I opened my eyes.
I listened closely because My God is wise.
"My dear daughter, you are such a joy to me,
My heart breaks when you don't see.

Do I need your help to make the world right?
Your presence here on earth and in this life
leaves you myopic with your limitations.
You can't know all available considerations.

I know with your heart, your faith, and trust.
You want me to act like you think I must.
The recommendations you speak
aren't wrong, but it's MY will You seek."

My Heavenly Father paused in his recitation.
The Holy Spirit helped with my communication.
"So Abba, Daddy, God, are you telling me
You only want me to agree?'

I love it when I get an important revelation.
He wants me to seek Him for information.
He is the only one who has all of the answers.
The creator of the universe is the planner.

So, it isn't about my trust or faith or ability,
or if I have the knowledge and the capability
to do the things that I'm responsible to do.
Dear Father, God, it is solely about You!

Photo 189162575 @ Michael Tatman / Dreamstime.com

June

Filters

Why is my hope so erratic? No. Hope is not unstable; my feelings and emotions are fickle. Where is the balance between living in hope and acknowledging hard?

One evening, I was in a good mood when I went to a writing class. The world was right with me then, and I was excited to meet with the group.

When I got there, I discovered one of the ladies' cancer had returned. Someone else had lost their job, and another person's parents were sick. I felt guilty for feeling good and didn't know what to do with the bad news I had heard. How does one hold on to the "good feelings" when there is so much sadness? What do we do with the sadness?

Scripture tells us to go to the Lord and give it to Him. Leave it at His feet because He is a big enough God that He can take care of all of us. We only have to give it up and leave it there. After we leave the burden at His feet, we are in a better position to hear how our good God wants us to encourage those who are hurting. Sometimes it is as small as us telling them how sorry we are, sometimes He asks us to pray for them, and there are times our Father wants us to walk with them for a season.

God gives His children the grace we need to manipulate through difficult times. He does not provide us with grace for someone else's challenges. We are commanded to share each other's burdens, which does not mean taking the entire load.

28 Come to me, all who labor and are heavy laden, and I will give you rest. 29 Take my yoke upon you, and learn from me, for I am gentle and lowly in heart, and you will find rest for your souls. 30 For my yoke is easy, and my burden light.

<u>**Isaiah 40:31 (NIV)**</u>

31 But those who hope in the Lord will renew their strength. They will soar on wings like eagles; they will run and not grow weary; they will walk and not be faint.

The only thing I can see is distress all around.
Contentment and peace can hardly be found.
How can I understand the reality of life?
Acknowledge the good and accept the strife.

I must learn to filter all I see
through the filters that God gives me.
The distorted filters I have in place now
I want to change but don't know how.

Jesus lived a hard life and died in shame,
but He doesn't view His life the same.
He wept when He was sad,
He cried out to the Father when it got bad.

If I'm to live my life as Jesus did
I must hear the wisdom the Holy Spirit gives.
The lies of the enemy must go away.
I want to focus on what God would say.

We've lived through the darkest day
when Jesus died and was put in a grave.
He did what He promised, and three days later,
the darkest day turned into something better.

An event that could only be from God,
the resurrection of His heavenly Son.
Since Jesus lives forevermore,
we need not worry about the world.

Thank you, Jesus, Holy Spirit, and Father,
I focus only on You; the rest is a bother.
Joy and peace are accessible in every way
if I only concentrate on what You say.

How Much Power Do Your Words Have?

Words. Can you imagine a world without words? Even in a society created by Science Fiction authors in which words are not spoken, they still communicate in words. The spoken word made the universe and everything in it. Spoken words determine the good and bad of a situation. The Bible even says in **John 1:1**, *"In the beginning was the Word and the Word was with God, and the Word was God."*

I've been studying and considering words lately. I've only recently accepted that my words hold more power than I can imagine. Since I was unaware of their power, it was easier to speak without saying anything. Not only saying empty words but saying hateful words or words that hurt … first us and then others …. can cause a shift in the universe. Let's consider how powerful words really are.

In the beginning, God saw a world void and without form. He decided to change all of that. How? With Words. "And God Said … And God Said …" and everything God said was so. Not only was it "so," it was all good, and when He created man, He declared that He made man in "His" own image, and it was "perfect."

We are created in God's image. It only makes sense that we have the capacity to love as God loves, but we must also realize the words we speak have as much power as God's words. Jesus attempted to let us know just how much power we have, which is the same power that the Triune has. Remember the parable of the mustard seed? This parable was impactful enough that it is contained in all three gospels! **(Matthew 13:31-32, Mark 4:30-32 and Luke 13:18-19).**

What would it look like if all of the people of God could grasp the significance of our availability to God's power? What about a true understanding of the power of our words? Might we change the declarations we make, and perhaps become more intentional about what we actually say?

Instead of coming against a situation that makes me uncomfortable, for instance, a social activity where I don't know anyone, I will say in the past I may have been anxious, but now I know I have nothing to fear because God's perfect love casts out all fear. I can face the unknown with God's strength. I will remember when I speak, I own what I say, and am actually prophesying the future. "It will probably rain the day we go to the beach." "I cannot do that because I will get sick", or any number of negative statements.

I'm not talking about the "name it, claim it" mentality. We can claim good things for ourselves, but the enemy, as he loves to do, distorts God's loving messages with lies. Our first course of action is to have a solid relationship with the Lord and an open line of conversation with Him. When we get our priorities in order, we are in a position to claim power over darkness. It doesn't mean all things will be good, it merely means we can walk through adversity with joy in our hearts, because we have the power to claim that "God is Good" and "All things work together for Good for those who love God and are called according to His purpose." **(Romans 8:28 NKV)**

<u>Proverbs 18:21 (NKJ)</u>
21 Death and life are in the power of the tongue, And those who love it will eat its fruit.

<u>**Proverbs 16:24 (NKJ)**</u>
*24 Pleasant words are like a honeycomb, Sweet to the soul
and healing to the bones.*

<u>**Matthew 12:37 (NKJ)**</u>
*37 For by your words you will be justified, and by your
words you will be condemned."*

God, my Heavenly Father in Heaven,
thank you for our salvation You have given.
But there is more to salvation than we know.
I want to understand everything You show.

When you were in this world,
all things heard and obeyed Your words.
Please help me to remember I have a choice
to proclaim Your truth with my voice.

I want my actions and the words I proclaim
to bring peace, not heartache and pain.
I often say words without thinking.
When I do, I see my spirit sinking.

I want to take captive every thought
and only say positive words you taught.
The words you spoke had deep meaning.
Everything was for the purpose of redeeming.

Thank You for all of the love you give,
thank You for showing me how to live,
to show myself approved by a good daddy.
Thank you for never giving up on me.

I Want to Heal … Don't I?

My Abba Father. What is stirring in my soul? What are you telling me, or what do you want to say to me? Holy Spirit … is there an assignment that I'm not seeing? Do you have something for me to do?

I'm still looking for validation from sources that aren't real. How do I realize and receive the Holy Spirit's assurance and have it be enough? Where does this urgency to be heard, acknowledged, and praised come from? Why does it always seem like the bottomless pit, and there is nothing to satiate the desire I have to be validated?

There is a closed room inside my heart that hasn't been opened for years. It is solidly shut, stuck, and rusted. No prying can open that door. I shut the door of that room a long time ago because what was inside was so painful and humiliating; I never want to experience the awfulness of that room ever again. I shut the door, locked it, hammered nails all around it, and used cement to ensure it never opened. I even painted it to appear like this door was just a continuation of the space in my heart.

Holy Spirit. That door has been a part of my life as long as before I can remember. I've done well keeping it together without facing that room. If I open it, whatever I'm hiding from will be revealed, and God, I don't think I want to have whatever it is flood my soul.

That room keeps me grounded in … I don't know anymore. It keeps me grounded, but why do I feel like I need to be grounded? Why can't I know so intimately the Holy Spirit to the point that I can take flight?

What will happen if I let go of the pain in that room, the decay, and the rot?

I don't know. I don't know and am unsure if I want to know. Yet, I think, Holy Spirit, you are telling me that I must open that door and let you inside so I can be totally free from the anchor it has on my soul. I never want to open that room, yet … that has to happen. If I want to experience the Holy Spirit's absolute fullness, that room must be opened and cleaned out by the Father.

2 Corinthians 7:8-10 (NLT)

*8 I am not sorry that I sent that severe letter to you, though I was sorry at first, for I know it was painful to you for a little while. 9 Now I am glad I sent it, not because it hurt you, but because the pain caused you to repent and change your ways. It was the kind of sorrow God wants his people to have, so you were not harmed by us in any way. 10 For **the kind of sorrow God wants us to experience leads us away from sin and results in salvation**. There's no regret for that kind of sorrow. But worldly sorrow, which lacks repentance, results in spiritual death.*

2 Corinthians 5:17 (NLT)

17 This means that anyone who belongs to Christ has become a new person. The old life is gone; a new life has begun!

Romans 7:15-17 (NIV)

15 I do not understand what I do. For what I want to do I do not do, but what I hate I do. 16 And if I do what I do not want to do, I agree that the law is good. 17 As it is, it is no longer I myself who do it, but it is sin living in me.

Tender hearts are crushed.
The brokenhearted are overlooked in the rush
of living life in a fallen world.
We know this and cry out to our Lord.

But when I cry out in pain
and feel the hurt, I go insane.
Instead of feeling and giving enough,
I refuse to accept it and choose to stuff.

So much is festering inside
it bleeds into my soul, and I hide.
I talk with a smile and put on a show
for those around me that I know.

My Heavenly Father is so good to me.
He refuses to give up until I'm free.
Yet I keep a place deep within
which stores my darkest sin.

It isn't the sin of doing something wrong.
It's a sin of omission which is strong
because it doesn't look so bad.
If left unconfessed, my countenance is sad.

What is this omission that fills my soul,
and keeps me feeling so low?
I think it's the fact that I don't truly release
the fear and bitterness stored deep beneath.

The darkness won't go away
no matter what good words others say.
How can I want something so badly?
Could I watch it disappear? Gladly!

Something inside refuses to release
completely – Father, why? Tell me, please.
I don't want my soul to be so submerged
in the muck – I want it purged.

Father, please take it from my heart,
not just the accessible areas, but every part.
I've been to this place many times before.
I get close to the deepest darkest door.

I'm on the verge of releasing it.
I try to unlock it, the key doesn't fit.
The disappointment that the door won't open
gives way to relief, I won't have to go in.

I won't have to face the hurtful things
of a lifetime of denial that my memories bring.
God, Holy Spirit, please tell me why
I refuse to let you get rid of the things I hide?

How do I ultimately convince myself
the memories are past. When I delve
into the ocean of brokenness and defeat,
I must realize my salvation is complete.

Jesus Christ loves me so much.
His sacrifice was for the places I can't touch.
I don't have to open that door
to something I've never seen before.

I tell The Holy Spirit that I will allow Him
to break the door down and go on in.
When I do that, finally, one day,
The Holy Spirit will take over without delay.

He will dig through the ruinous rotten things
and purge all of the hardness that brings
me to places I go alone to hide,
so no one will know what's inside.

But my Heavenly Father wants me to know
that He doesn't care how dark and low
the sin of my bitterness or deepest regret.
He will be the one to take and purge all of it.

My Abba, Father, Daddy, and God
constantly wait for my approval nod.
What will my life look like
if I let the Holy Spirit clean inside?

This is a concept I've never known.
But I want to be ready to be shown.

It's Time to Get Serious

I'm not perfect. I know that because the only reason I am a daughter of the King is because of Jesus Christ and His sacrifice. No. I'm not perfect. I wasn't born perfect because I was born to my biological father, and no good is found in him. God is bigger than my sin. He is bigger than my circumstances, and He is bigger than the universe because He is all, and without Him, there is nothing.

Assuredly, I'm not perfect. It isn't difficult to say I'm not perfect. I can say that all day long. I have difficulty saying … I have done and said things that my Father wants me to confess and repent from. If I begin with specifics about something I want to change, then my soul must agree with what I know, that I'm not perfect. As long as my soul thinks I'm perfect, then how can I confess and repent of things in my life that aren't perfect? As long as I don't confess and repent, I leave little room for my Father's light and adoration.

I'm not saying that my Father withholds His light and adoration from me; I just don't have room to receive it because I'm full of unconfessed trash I've been hoarding. I suppose it would be likened unto lukewarm. It's there; I don't do anything about it, but I don't act on it, so it stagnates. Unrepentance leads to stagnation. Again, not because my Father withholds anything from me. However, unless I agree with Him and His thoughts about me, they cannot comfort me or give me the light in my spirit that is meant to be my strength.

Isaiah 50: 2-3 (NLT)
2 Why was no one there when I came? Why didn't anyone answer when I called? Is it because I have no power to rescue? No, that is not the reason! For I can speak to the sea

and make it dry up! I can turn rivers into deserts covered with dying fish. 3 I dress the skies in darkness covering them with clothes of mourning.

Isaiah 49: 3-4 (NLT)
3 He said to me, "You are my servant, Israel, and you will bring me glory." 4 I replied, "But my work seems so useless! I have spent my strength for nothing and to no purpose. ... Yet I leave it all in the Lord's hand; I will trust God for my reward."

God, even in the darkest night
You bring comfort amid my plights.
You keep me steady with Your right hand.
With the strength you give me, I can stand.

There are times I get downcast.
Usually, because I meander into my past
and look at all the bad of my life,
which puts me into mourning my strife.

The truth is, Lord, the past is long gone
and doesn't apply to today. I must go on.
I can accomplish what You want me to
only if I focus on what is good and true.

The unfailing truth Father God,
is that You have given me Your nod
to live this life in victory
because the sacrifice of Your Son set me free.

So, Holy Spirit, come into my heart.
Clean and polish out all of the dark
that I have stuffed way deep inside.
I don't want to provide hurt a place to hide.

Fill every part, even those forgot about.
Fill me with so much light; I want to shout
and declare to everyone around me
how great it is to finally be free.

Please, Comforter, bring to my memory
things that are stagnant and way down deep,
so I can finally give up whatever you decide
I should confess and repent and not hide.

Photo 159489651 @ Wirestock / Dreamstime.com

July

Independence Day

We are ready to celebrate one of the first holidays in our country. Our country is a combination of immigrants. The only natives are the Native-American Indians. We came together, pooled all of our independence, and forged it into what is now the United States of America.

Do we have troubles? Sure. There is turmoil, greed, and self-interest. We get disgusted, but at the end of the day, we are still a proud and free people.

Recently I've heard it said that nobody cares about History anymore. Maybe that's true. I think about History because that is where pride in my country comes from. Our country was founded by rebels who believed in freedom not offered in any other country. Against all odds, the rebels succeeded in breaking from oppression.

If we go back in History and trace the path we've taken, we see that we are slowly instituting the same constraints we fought to overcome.

History shows a pattern, the same pattern, the same road which leads to destruction. If we paid close attention to History, would we perhaps learn from the mistakes of others and dodge the destructive road?

I don't know. I think about how our wars destroyed thousands of people's lives, demolished entire towns or villages, and crushed nature. When the United States is involved in destruction, after the dust settles, we generously assist in rebuilding what we destroyed.

History shows we are imperfect people trying to create a perfect world. The primary factor in our troubles directly correlates to God being removed from places of importance.

There is a reduction in morals, honor, and consideration for our fellow persons.

Yes, we have problems. Yes, we are in chaos, but for now, we can still celebrate our Independence Day and enjoy the freedom of how we celebrate. Today we can still go to church unencumbered by persecution. For now, we are still the United States of America … Land of the free! For now, we can sleep uninterrupted by the fear of bombs.

Galatians 5:1 (NIV)
1 It is for freedom that Christ has set us free. Stand firm, then, and do not let ourselves be burdened again by a yoke of slavery.

Galatians 5:13 (NIV)
13 You, my brothers and sisters, were called to be free. But do not use your freedom to indulge the flesh; rather, keep one another humbly in love

Today, we celebrate a land of freedom for all.
Shall we enjoy our freedom before we fall?
Our celebration will look like destruction.
Tomorrow we'll return to our dissatisfactions.

But today, we share gratefulness for freedom.
Today let's show our goodwill to someone.
While we still can, shall we shine God's light
so maybe we can keep us from plunging into the night?

Freedom Redefined

The days we live in are lovely, aren't they? Pandemic aside, I am a sixty-five-year-old grandmother using technology that didn't exist when I was born. I speak to more people than I will ever meet about something dear to my heart.

We are in recovery after almost three years of disruption from life because of the global pandemic of 2020. It's time for us to step back from the midst of terror and look at reality.

We are part of a great country living here in the United States. Our freedom allows us to close businesses or not, to isolate or not, to wash our hands. Americans value our freedom, but we have forgotten one thing. Freedom is only as safe as the people who protect it. And my freedom ends where someone else's begins.

What freedom isn't is politics; freedom is inclusive, considerate of others, and responsible. Politics is divisive, elitist, selfish, and burdens those who would make America stronger. As a nation, we have allowed politics to dictate who we are and how we respond.

Politics is not a proponent of people. Politicians don't respect the people they represent, and they are using us as pawns in their power games. They pretend to be our friends and stab us in the back the minute we turn. Who in leadership really gives a hoot about us trying to do the responsible thing when there is clearly a disconnect in what the responsible thing is.

We have a wealth of information available at our fingertips. I personally have read articles, blogs, Facebook entries to follow the progress of this pandemic. The media and the public reports are territorial, and separating fact from fabricated fact is not easy.

Despite the pandemic, people are born, get married, love, hate, die, and live. Nothing has changed except someone yelled out one day "The Sky is Falling" and panicked the world. I daresay, more people die by acting in a panic than the tragedy itself. Have you seen what happens in an enclosed structure with two doors for hundreds of people when a fire breaks out?

 We value our lives and rush to get out first. If everyone did the right thing, helped those who needed it, made sure each one got their chance to get out of the door instead of blocking it, trampling each other because of the push and shove to get out, if we would just be courteous, most of us would make it through a disaster intact.

I don't have the answers. All I have is a heart and love for my country and everyone in my life, and everyone who hears me. I'm concerned because when this is over, and it will be over, will we be able to look our neighbor in the eyes and smile at them because we did what was right? Are we going to be able to tell our grandchildren we were able to survive the pandemic and keep our humanity? We have to live with the fallout of all that is happening. Not the president, not the CDC, not Congress … each of us individually. It is up to us to make the fallout as painless as possible.

We don't need more laws to show us how to live. If the majority would adhere to the two great commandments; "Love the Lord your God with all your might, with all your heart and with all your soul", and the second right up there with the first; "Love your neighbor as yourself." Yes, God even tells us it is okay to love ourselves and do things that are good for us, but remember when we do, we are compelled to treat others just like that. What would our community look like if we took these two commandments to heart?

I may only be one person, and one person cannot do much, but no matter what, I will do what I can to make a difference for those close to me. What about you? Will you join me to set our country right again? Will you take this consideration for others to your community and be a positive example? Take care, stay safe and be practical.

<u>Mark 12:30- 31 (NLT)</u>

30 And You must love the Lord your God with all your heart, all your soul, all your mind, and all your strength. 31 The second is equally important: 'Love your neighbor as yourself.' No other commandment is greater than these.

<u>Galatians 5:13 (NIV)</u>

13 You, my brothers, and sisters, were called to be free. But do not use your freedom to indulge the flesh; rather, serve one another humbly in love.

<u>Habakkuk 1:4 (NLT)</u>

4 The law has become paralyzed and there is no justice in the courts. The wicked far outnumber the righteous, so that justice has become perverted.

We rang in 2020, celebrating another new year
with lots of laughter, good times and cheer.
It did not take long for everyone to see
we should have started this year differently.

Chaos is a common state in our world,
but it got out of control with each word.
Don't go out in public or hug each other.
Close everything down said the government.

If we isolate, we will get through this.
Days passed and we began to ask what if …
our isolation only caused this crisis to double.
But it caused more depression and trouble,

more irritability, impatience and intolerance.
Soon, the virus was replaced by violence.
Rage and hatred took over our land,
and indeed, everything got out of hand.

We were taught as children early on,
wash our hands and let the dirt be gone.
Cover your mouth if you cough or sneeze.
Keep your hands away from your face please.

Stay home if you are sick.
If you get worse, go to the doctor quick.
Do not carry your illness to parties or work,
take care of yourself; we learned this at birth.

Notice others, and if someone is in need,
do what you can and help them succeed.
Encourage them with clothes, or food.
Give from your blessings to those with few.

Our isolation turned some of us to destruction
as we wallowed in despair and frustration.
Kindness hid when we stayed in our homes
thinking we had to survive on our own.

Our graduating seniors suffered a lot.
No celebrating the years they were taught.
They were not able to gather as a class
or dream about how their future would pass.

After all this despair is there any more hope?
What is out there for us to help us cope?
Who is capable of spreading a little cheer,
to us and to those we love and hold dear?

The answer is as old as God's creation.
He has the ability to stop the destruction.
He doesn't use fanfare, trumpets, and noise.
He quietly uses His church to spread joy.

The church did not take a vacation from life.
They invented new ways to shine God's light.
They provided encouragement,
and reminded us, we are not all that different.

We must connect to each other,
our family, friends, sisters, and brothers.
We cannot ignore our need for interactions.
When we do, there's hatred and frustration.

God does not want us to isolate from our life.
He wants us to spread His goodness and light
to a lost world living in all this chaos.
He reminds us to give joy for what we lost.

Thank you to the many health professionals
who tirelessly served without hesitation.
To the peacekeepers who came out in force
and everyone who continued the course.

Remember this, at the end of everything,
God is in control, and His will is to redeem
those who believe His words and accept
His salvation and His love will not quit.

So, in summation, we have a choice
in our actions. Will we cry or rejoice?
I choose to not allow the bad news we hear
to defeat me. Instead, I will spread Cheer.

Our God and Government

We live in a time when the loudest political message is one of corruption, and this knowledge brings despair to my soul. The people who decide what my life will look like care nothing about me. The decisions they make are not made for the purpose of a better world.

I read Daniel and heard the message that God is the one who sets kings and presidents in office, as well as all of the other government officials. How am I supposed to react to that knowledge? What do scriptures tell me about my responsibilities to government officials? Grudgingly, I answer my question because my responsibilities include respect, honor, obedience (unless it goes against God's laws), and uplifting them in prayer.

Difficult? Of course, it is, and I was in the middle of discussing my revelation in my spirit when the Holy Spirit interrupted my musing with a familiar name; "David."

God anointed Saul as king, but after his disobedience and pride, God took his anointing away and commanded Samuel to anoint David as king. God's plans are good, but He also gives us free will to make decisions, and sometimes those decisions are contrary to His desire for us. Consequently, Saul did not step down from his position and, for thirteen years, pursued David to kill him.

What was David's response? The only time David did anything adverse to Saul's action was when he cut off a corner of the King's robe. But he confessed and repented almost as soon as he did it. From the time Saul was anointed king until after he died, David respected Saul and chastised those who would harm or disrespect him.

So, I asked myself again; "what is a godly response to our corrupt government officials? Obey, respect, and most importantly, thank God for HIS sovereignty and pray for their protection, wisdom, and discernment."

Can we commit to praying for our government officials? After all, God is in the business of changing circumstances and hearts.

Daniel 2:21-22 (NIV84)

21 "He changes times and seasons; He sets up kings and deposes them. He gives wisdom to the wise and knowledge to the discerning. 22 He reveals deep and hidden things; He knows what lies in darkness, and light dwells with Him.

Romans 13: 1-2 (NIV)

1 Let everyone be subject to the governing authorities, for there is no authority except that which God has established. The authorities that exist have been established by God. 2 Consequently, whoever rebels against the authority is rebelling against what God has instituted, and those who do so will bring judgment on themselves.

Sometimes I realize God's mandates are hard,
especially when I think they are marred.
Yet God is Truth, and His word still stands
even when we don't understand.

I complained about our government one day
and advised God on the best way
for Him to make our country right.
Remove today's governments from our sight!

If He did, then maybe His followers here
would get involved and elect people who care
about God's laws and fix immorality today.
Then I sat back to hear what he would say.

Imagine my surprise when he reminded me
that He is in control of everything I see,
those who sit in office and on our courts.
Even those who support the corrupt.

"But God, why do you choose
to allow these unethical people to rule.
Chaos and turmoil and unrest fill our days
as each official selfishly promotes their way."

The Holy Spirit is wise beyond what I know.
He eternity, past and future, to show
how little we grasp in our mind
because our current existence is too finite.

Once again, the lesson for me to learn
is to have faith and trust our God to discern
the truth of this life and the plans He made.
I must obey Him and not be swayed.

At the end of time, the world will be right.
Our troubles will pass; and so will our plight,
and difficult times while in the world today.
All will be right with us when we obey.

God Fights for Us

Maybe you are going through a dark season of your life right now. It is possibly not as dark as it has been, or even as dark as you may see in the future, but right now, it feels never-ending.

Daily, we fight a Goliath of the same proportion as the giant David faced. Saul wanted to force his armor, the world's weapons, upon David. The God-given wisdom bestowed on David allowed him to recognize the difference between God's protection and man's protection. Man's weapons and protection looked more powerful, and indeed Goliath had all of the best weapons the world had to offer, but David knew where his real power came from. Our heavenly Father, who spoke the world into existence, gives us what we need to overcome the world because it is His fight, not ours.

David removed Saul's best protection, put down the most potent weapons, and took up his slingshot and some rocks. With his head held high, he walked out in his sandals and tunic, faced the insurmountable enemy of God, and allowed all of God's power to push through, and the giant fell for good!

Thank You, Lord! I will not look at the difficulty of living at this moment. My eyes are not fixed upon the waves of adversity … I see My God, and the Holy Spirit fills me with all I need to overcome today.

Ephesians 6:10-12 (NIV)
10 Finally, be strong in the Lord and in His mighty power. 11 Put on the full armor of God, so that you can take your stand against the devil's schemes. 12 For our struggle is not

against flesh and blood, but against the rulers, against the authorities, against the powers of this dark world and against the spiritual forces of evil in the heavenly realms.

<u>Philippians 4:7 (NIV)</u>
4 And the peace of God, which transcends all understanding, will guard your hearts and your minds in Christ Jesus.

<u>Hebrews 12:2 (NIV)</u>
2 Let us keep looking to Jesus. Our faith comes from Him, and He is the One Who makes it perfect. He did not give up when He had to suffer shame and die on a cross. He knew of the joy that would be His later. Now He is sitting at the right side of God.

How can I ever doubt the goodness of God!
He created us so He can pour out His love.
Even when He knew how we would rebel,
with His arms around us, we are forever held.

The Father endured the heartache
of asking His only Son to take
the penalty we deserved because of our sin.
God's grace allows us to start over again.

No matter what life throws at me,
and despite all the evil, I can see
there is a vast army of Angels all around
who are there to have the enemy bound.

There is absolutely nothing in this life,
no hardship, no pain, no devastation, no strife
that my good God does not know about.
He can destroy them I have no doubt.

God is gathering His people even now
for victory; we don't know how.
People of God, lift your banner high
because the end of the enemy is nigh.

Then our Lord God, Holy Spirit, and Savior
will call His bride and cast her His favor.
Nothing we've endured in our time
will stand against the goodness of the divine.
So dear children of the Most High King,
gather together, lift your hands and sing!

Photo 834787 @ Peter Dolinsky / Dreamstime.com

August

Living Above the Pain

My granddaughter received a Yorkipoo puppy for her ninth birthday. She named him Oreo because he was black with a spot of white on his chest. His training was a family affair – my granddaughter, her mother, and I – because puppies are about as exhausting as a baby. It didn't take him long to steal the family's heart. Oh, he was the cutest and sweetest, coming into his own. He loved to be cuddled.

My daughter and granddaughter left town, and I took care of Oreo. That night he got sick. Since he was so tiny, I knew any loss of fluid could be dangerous, so I called the vet, and he said to bring him in the following day. He suspected Oreo had swallowed something that obstructed his bowels.

That morning he had surgery to remove a blockage he didn't have, so the next diagnosis was parvo. He was hospitalized, and two days later, we lost him. They said he probably didn't have parvo but rather distemper. He didn't get sick because we neglected his shots. He just hadn't finished the regime. My granddaughter and I were with him when he died. We both cried and said our goodbyes. It was heartbreaking.

When my sister responded to the news that we lost little Oreo, she made a profound statement. To paraphrase, she said that she had to believe that the hurt we experience will make us stronger. Not in areas we might expect, but God will use the pain to grow and stretch us in ways He needs us to grow. With the encouragement of God's Word, we must always live above our hurts, disappointments, and failures. They will be there always, but somehow, we can live higher than where they are. I still miss that little puppy two years later!

<u>Ecclesiastes 7:3-4 (NLT)</u>
3 Sorrow is better than laughter, for sadness has a refining influence on us. 4 A wise person thinks a lot about death, while a fool thinks only about having a good time.

<u>2 Corinthians 1:4 (NLT)</u>
4 He comforts us in all our troubles so that we comfort others. When they are troubled, we will be able to give them the same comfort God has given us.

<u>Matthew 5:4 (NLT)</u>
4 God blesses those who mourn, for they will be comforted.

When I was a child, warm and well fed,
with two caring parents and a warm, soft bed.
Life was good, and the sun shone brightly
until the day was over, and then it was night.

It wasn't long before storm clouds came.
After that nothing was the same.
It isn't fair for a child of just a few years
To see the harshness of life full of fears.

My family faced one tragedy after another;
me, my parents, sisters, and brothers.
The chaos of all the storms we faced
made it seem like bad was winning the race.

I grew from a child to a responsible adult
weighed down by trials and sad results.
My cries no longer were heard out loud.
I learned such reactions were not allowed.

Pretending my life was something it wasn't
consumed my energy until I was inefficient
to maneuver the routine ups and downs
causing the bad to be ultimately profound.

My desire was to have the joy unsurpassed,
the kind that God tells us is ours, but alas,
I didn't know how to work with what I had.
I didn't see that the good outweighed the bad.

I wanted answers to the questions I asked.
I longed for the sunshine, so I could bask
in the comfort of peace, a mission I pursued.
I used all of me, until I had nothing to use.

One time in an email from my sister, she said
no one can ever escape pain, but instead
of allowing the hurt to make us insane,
it's best to learn to live above all the pain.

Simple words, easy to say but profound!
After years of searching, I finally found
wisdom in her answer, but I question now,
who can I talk with to help me understand how?

Of course, I've known the answer all along,
but the mind isn't where this truth belongs.
The mind is flesh, this knowledge is meant
for the spirit so no one can circumvent.

I dug through years of sludge to create a way
for the words to slide into the heart to stay,
the words I heard were from our Father.
He's the reason our pain makes us stronger.

When we see what is going on around us,
we get caught in the actions of the traitorous.
Raising our eyes to God's higher plane
helps us to live above the pain.

I Am Loved and Cherished

I remember the first time I understood just a tiny bit about God's love for me. God's love is elusive for those who learned about our God through a legalistic perspective. God's grace and love cannot co-exist with the pharisaical laws of legalism.

At the beginning of my journey into freedom, God gave me a godly Christian woman as my mentor. During one of our visits, she told me that God loves me so much he sings over me. I had never heard of such a thing and couldn't believe her. Then she showed me a passage in Zephaniah. How could a God who demands perfection sing anything joyful over me when I could not get living for God right?

No matter what I did in my life, I just wasn't happy. I was depressed, and I couldn't project the joy of the Lord. Reading the message from God through the inspired words written by Zephaniah was one of the catalysts which started me on my journey to freedom.

<u>Zephaniah 3:17 (ESV)</u>
17 The Lord, your God, is in your midst, a mighty one who will save; he will rejoice over you with gladness; he will quiet you by his love; he will exult over you with loud singing.

<u>1st Peter 2:9 (NIV)</u>
9 but you are a chosen people, a royal priesthood, a holy nation, God's special possession, that you may declare the praises of him who called you out of darkness into his wonderful light.

I was sitting with my Father today,
waiting to hear what He might say.
Often times I am completely surprised
by the way He speaks so clearly inside.

The quiet voice of the Holy Spirit
can get kind of loud until I hear it;
the message He has for me.
He refuses to stop until I finally see.

I was recently awed by a truth I never knew.
God's love for me was so strong He pursued
me through all of the years of my life.
His desire was to take on my strife.

I've spent many years looking for His favor
by trying to guess how to adjust my behavior.
Doing good things looking for His approval,
and repenting when I felt like a failure.

Now I realize how much He loves me.
His desire is for my spirit to be set free,
and let the spirit's wisdom keep me safe;
let Him lead me to a special place.

The place isn't a geographical location.
It's an internal acceptance of His inspiration.
All of these years, I've tried to do it alone.
God already knew everything I'd sewn.

I marvel at His patience and care,
even when I thought He wasn't there.
Now I can look back on my life and see
how much He has always cared for me.

This new revelation is so grand
and something beyond what I can understand.
The enemy is determined to take me down,
but I have God's protection all around.

Yet when I remember the truths of His Word,
I refuse to let the enemy disturb
the peace my Father so freely gives
to me, and I remember He's the reason I live.

God's Name for You

Just as our earthly parents named us, so has our Heavenly Father. I've never thought about that concept before or given it much power. About three years ago, I was at a conference, and one of the exercises was to close our eyes and pray for God to reveal His name for us. The minute I closed my eyes, even before I asked the Holy Spirit to tell my name, one came to mind. Of course, I discounted it, sure that I was the one who came up with the name. Now that I think about the word I heard – Radiant – it wasn't something I would ever choose to call myself, so why would I come up with this name on my own?

Dictionary.com provides the following definition of "Radiant."

Adjective

1. *emitting rays of light; shining; bright: the radiant sun; radiant colors.*
2. *bright with joy, hope, etc.: radiant smiles; a radiant future.*

Who am I to question the name God gave to me? Take time out of your life to sit with the Holy Spirit and ask Him what your new name is. Accept the word He gives you. Don't be like I was, questioning the name He chose. God knows us more intimately than we know ourselves because, after all, as David said, *"He knitted us together in our mother's womb."* **(Psalm 139:13)**

Isaiah 62: 1-2 (ESV)
1 For Zion's sake I will not keep silent, and for Jerusalem's sake I will not be quiet, until her righteousness goes forth as

*brightness, and her salvation as a burning torch. **2** The nations shall see your righteousness, and all the kings your glory, and you shall be called by a new name that the mouth of the Lord will give.*

Isaiah 49:16 (ESV)
***16** Behold, I have engraved you on the palms of my hands; your walls are continually before me.*

Psalm 54:4 & 5 (ESV)

***4** I prayed to the Lord, and He answered me. He freed me from all my fears. **5** Those who look to Him for help will be* **radiant with joy**. *No shadow of shame will darken their faces.*

God has a name for everyone.
He created and loved us before time began.
So, logically thinking about His love,
why wouldn't He name us from above?

When we were born to a mom and dad,
they named us, maybe good maybe bad.
The enemy found ways to destroy us,
through thoughts that would cause us to fuss.

The enemy's lies caused me to create labels,
and these names told me that I wasn't able
to do anything. My feelings were distorted,
his lies rang true, but they weren't supported.

There was one time I sat with God
in a group of women being taught
about the great love He has for us.
He wants to keep us close and snug.

The speaker told us to close our eyes
and reminded us God does not disguise
how much He cares and loves us all.
He picks us up every time we fall.

She told us to listen for the unique name
God gave to us, which offsets our shame.
Before I even got both eyes closed
I was surprised by the name God disclosed.

The name he gave me initially
was one I'd never considered; Radiant.
His answer too quickly came,
So, I tried to think of another name.

To my chagrin, God is more stubborn than I.
He said I am radiant as the stars in the sky.
Again, today I spent time with God.
For once, I didn't have a desire to nod off.

God showed me a verse in *the Psalms.*
Psalm thirty-four, verse five is like a song.
His word told me when I look to Him
during the hard times when things look grim,

His grace and power will fill my space
and His radiance will shine on my face.
Thank You, Lord, for speaking to me
the truth You have taught me to believe.

Holy Spirit - God In Us
When Life Is Hard

Many years ago, when I was young, life was easy, at least from a child's perspective. Let's think about it for a moment. For the most part, when we are born, someone is always there to take care of our needs, and indeed our needs are few. All we ask is for our belly to be full, our diapers to be clean, and loving arms to comfort us when we need them. Parents love us even when we don't ***do*** anything, we just are, and they enjoy our presence.

God's revelation to us never comes all at once because His goodness would be so powerful that we would run. Exodus Chapters 19 and 20 records Moses' conversations with God at different times. God wanted to meet His people personally, but He had to put parameters because they could not see His total holiness, or they would die. In the end, in Exodus 20:20 -21, they begged Moses to give them God's message himself because they feared God too much to get close.

The Holy Spirit is God in us. Think about the magnificence of that! Constant access to the God who transcends space and time, the creator of all! Because of Jesus and His willingness to be an atonement for our sins, God is always with us.

<u>**2 Corinthians 1:21-22 (God's Word Translation)**</u>

21 God establishes us, together with you, in a relationship with Christ. He has also anointed us. 22 In addition, he has put his seal of ownership on us and has given us the Spirit as his guarantee.

<u>**Deuteronomy 31:5 (NIV)**</u>
5 Be strong and courageous. Do not be afraid or terrified because of them, for the Lord your God goes with you; He will never leave you or forsake you.

<u>**John 14:26-27 (NIV)**</u>
26 But the Advocate, the Holy Spirit, whom the Father will send in my name, will teach you all things and will remind you of everything I have said to you. 27 Peace I leave with you; my peace I give you. I do not give to you as the world gives. Do not let your hearts be troubled, and do not be afraid.

When I was young, God was so big,
I never questioned anything He did.
A few years later, He wasn't any smaller,
and I saw things that made me wonder.

When in my teens I believed what I heard;
God was harsh, His goodness must be earned.
I tried to be perfect every hour
because, after all, I had access to His power.

We can count on turmoil and strife,
hard times and heartache in this life.
I always thought, though, if I was good
God would bless me because He could.

I became an adult and without my footing,
in a life wrought with minefields just waiting
to blow up and create a path with debris,
so much so that everyone could see.

Though I hid it well, I was sad.
After a while, I couldn't pretend to be glad.
I wanted to understand everything I could
about a God I wanted to believe was good.

The ups and downs of life are nothing new.
Good and bad came in as the wind blew.
I wanted to have what the Bible said –
the abundant life, I didn't believe what I read.

So, I kept asking – What's wrong with me?
Someone, tell me something I can see.
My life went on this way for years.
Nothing was different despite my tears.

In my head, I knew God loved me so much.
He wants to bless me with a gentle touch.
But I could never find the correct key,
so I decided this would always be.

Because God is perfect and loves me so,
He never left me – waiting for me to show
I could hear the truth about His character and
separate everything that wasn't His plan.

God led me to someone with a steady heart.
She was determined to show me how to start
to understand the truth of how God saw me.
How He yearned to release me to be free.

This anointed person He gave, and I
kept working through lows and highs.
She never gave up, always believed someday
I would understand, and I would see the way.

I did – I finally understood,
God believes that I am good!
Not because of anything I do.
He just loves me, and He's never through.

The only requirement He has for me
is to love Him and for me to be
constantly in communion with Him.
Because of Jesus – He sees no sin.

It seemed, but it wasn't – overnight
I went to bed with nothing right.
But when I woke for the very first time
I was able to feel God's beautiful sunshine.

Thank you, Father, for loving me so,
and loving and loving until I could know
everything in this life, good or bad
is moot. Your love I have always had.

Photo 44261734 @ Sanja Baljkas / Dreamstime.com

September

The Mystery of Chronic Bondage

Rebellion. Am I rebelling against becoming free? I mean totally free. Why would I do that?

I see a girl – a lone little girl sitting on a hill. The wind is whipping her long blond hair all around her face. Still, she sits and stares into a scene only she can see. Her expression is that of someone who was abandoned long ago. What does she see that has her desperate? Whatever she sees, it strikes terror in her soul.

I see a little girl that isn't so little anymore. Still, she sits alone on a hill with the wind whipping her long blonde hair around her face. Terror has been replaced with hopelessness. My heart breaks when I see her sad, empty, and cold. She still stares at a scene that leaves her soul open. She is ready to collapse in on herself.

I know she cries out because for as long as she can remember, this scene – whatever it is – has become death to her.

A dead-weighted horror that penetrates
her memories.

I see a young lady sitting in an office
staring into the face of despair.

Fear keeps me in rebellion. I don't know what totally free
would look like. I'm afraid I won't know what to do. But –
Fear is not of my Father. Fear is a tool the enemy uses to
keep us in bondage. **...** *" (I John 4:18 NIV) There is no fear
in love. But perfect love drives out fear,* and my Father,
God, Lord, and Savior are perfect love.

I am chosen – God's own special possession. He called me
out of darkness into the light. I am a new person living a new
life in Jesus and no longer a slave to sin but a daughter of
righteousness. As His child, I am chosen in Christ and holy
and without fault in God's eyes. Today at this moment in this
place, I choose to believe that God wants to meet me here.
He wants to talk to me and set me totally free. The right time
is now! Today is my day.

John 8:32 (ESV)
*32 And you will know the truth, and the truth will set you
free.*

John 8:34 (NASB)
*34 Jesus answered them, "Truly, truly, I say to you, everyone
who commits sin is the slave of sin.
"*

2 Timothy 1:7 (ESV)
*1 For God gave us a spirit not of fear but of power and love
and self-control.*

What is behind that closed door of mine?
I locked, nailed, glued it and left it behind.
I've done everything I can do
to get well, get free, live a life brand new.

Everything except to face this closed door.
It's a mystery, I don't know what's stored.
I've ignored it and pretended it wasn't there.
I told myself whatever is there, I don't care.

That door has been insignificant in the past.
I had so much to work through, and
a lifetime of healing from those wounds.
I ignored the door and what I now must do.

For the last few weeks now
I've had a restlessness. I've not known how
to determine why or where it's from.
Today, I heard the Holy Spirit say – come.

At first, I didn't hear the command clearly,
I clung to the unrest and held on dearly.
I didn't want to understand or even face
what I might have to look at and replace.

During my weekly Bible study, on a whim,
I confessed my fear to these Godly Women.
They listened to my story of lament
and kindly spoke words the Holy Spirit sent.

One friend confirmed she saw much fear.
She spoke words over me; she's such a dear.
She was gentle, but she didn't stop there.
She reminded me how much the Father cares.

Holy Spirit knows what's behind that door.
He wants to remove and see the trash no more.
No more heartache, sadness, and pain,
only the Father's love for me to retain.

Once that room has been cleaned up
I will never again allow the lies to interrupt
the joy He has planted in my heart.
My life, in complete freedom, can start.

I Found It!

Trust is the key to experiencing the fullness of the Holy Spirit. Even more than that, it is the key to living a life content in all circumstances. I recently received this realization, and when I could grasp the significance of the idea, an entirely new world opened up for me.

The world I had been living in was filled with suspicion and walls. I put up barriers to protect myself from harm and the pain of abandonment. I didn't feel protected when I was a child, so I developed this wall-building expertise as a survival tactic.

The secret about survival tactics one develops as a child is that they are not always the healthiest, even though they are necessary at the time. The enemy intends for those childhood survival strategies to take over before we think. If we analyze them as adults in light of who we are in Christ (The children of the Most High King), we may discard them for a better way.

I finally found" a better way. Trust in the Lord! He is the never-changing God of the universe and galaxies, so He has the power to take care of us. He doesn't promise a trouble-free life, but because I understand His love and the plans He has for me, I can take His truth and rest in it. My Great God can make good out of whatever befalls me, good or bad, and I will prosper by His protection.

Prosperity concerning God's kingdom, not the world. To live with the peace that passes all understanding, our perspective must be viewed as God's perspective, which is eternity.

<u>**Micah 7:5-7 (ESV)**</u>
5 Put no trust in a neighbor; have no confidence in a friend; guard the doors of your mouth from her who lies in your arms. 6 for the son treats the father with contempt, the daughter rises up against her mother, the daughter-in-law against her mother-in-law; a man's enemies are the men of his own house. 7 But as for me, I will look to the LORD; I will wait for the God of my salvation; my God will hear me.

<u>**Proverbs 3:5 (ESV)**</u>
5 Trust in the LORD with all your heart, and do not lean on your own understanding.

It was a little word, among so many,
which showed me joy when I didn't have any.
All of my life, I've searched the world,
looking for the secret to be unfurled.

From the start, darkness has been with me,
and as I got older, I knew I wasn't really free.
I heard from family, preachers, and teachers,
the answers with special procedures.

I probably tried everything I was taught,
and even researched but it was for naught.
I knew I loved the Lord my God,
He loved me, but I felt like a fraud.

I saw what I thought was a life exclusive
to Children of God, but alas, it was elusive.
There were times I climbed out of the abyss,
but the joy didn't last; something was amiss.

I know happiness does not produce joy.
Hardships come, happiness is destroyed.
Joy stays inside of us and never disappears.
The Love of The Lord casts out all fears.

Logically, I attempted to dissect my life,
to understand the sadness I had and why.
I spoke with pastors, wisdom I sought,
I read books to learn all I ought.

I reasoned through all of the hardships I faced.
Not only that, I attempted to trace
back to that one moment in time
I lost the joy that was supposed to be mine.

After many years of searching the cosmos
there were times I can honestly say I almost
had the answer on the tip of my knowledge
but it slipped away before it was solid.

I sat across from another therapist of my choice.
She knew things that I never voiced.
I learned what God sought from me
and all of the truths I knew but could not see.

Then one day, I asked her to explain why
people around me sensed I was hostile.
She turned the question around to me
and urged me to look honestly and deeply.

I didn't admit to any hostility per se,
but said I didn't trust and couldn't see a way
to overcome the intense feelings of distrust.
Her countenance told me all there was.

She asked the obvious in her opinion.
(Of course, I could think of a million.)
She made an interesting observation: we must
honestly ask often, Who do I trust?

My brow wrinkled with my question.
She was quick to interrupt with a suggestion.
Who do you belong to, and in whose arms?
Who promises to save you from harm?

"Oh, you mean God. My Heavenly Father?
The king of the Universe and even farther?"
That was the answer, but she clarified,
If you trust God, something is verified.

I began to understand as the lesson went on.
If I truly accept to whom I belong,
I will accept His love and no longer fear.
I hear His promise to wipe away my tears.

She suggested something I never thought of,
Ask your people to send prayers above
on my behalf so I don't do it alone.
(I tend to hold back because of the unknown.)

I heeded her suggestion and asked friends
who would pray for me and not just pretend.
I woke one morning to a brand-new world.
Not the newness I've experienced before.

This time the restlessness was gone.
There was no darkness to interrupt my song.
I couldn't believe and never understood
the contentment, but oh, it was good.

The joy I had always thought I had
would sometimes show me how to be glad.
But this? I had never experienced it before.
Darkness and heaviness were no more!

Oh, to give everyone
this feeling and knowledge that I belong.
This peace not of this world, I can say
that from now until I go home, is here to stay.

There Is No Door!

Depression had been a part of my life; I had almost given up hope of truly conquering it. I've had hours of therapy from numerous therapists. I had some time when the depression was lifted, but never for long. I had concluded I would never figure out what was wrong with me or what I was doing wrong. My good God never let me stop pursuing healing from this malady.

On one visit to a new therapist, I summarized my past and how I couldn't figure out how to get "fixed." She made a statement that changed my paradigm. She said: "What if you aren't really broken? What if you are what God intended, but you've been listening to what others thought you should be? You believed their opinions and, lost yourself."

I went home and processed her words. That was my first step on the path to freedom. I began to learn how my Heavenly Father loves me and my true identity as He defines it.

I also learned a valuable lesson from a story told by a wise person at a women's night at my church. The story was about an incident in her life that caused her fear of something. One day she talked to her mother about it and found out it didn't happen the way she remembered it.

I realized that the enemy … Satan is the master of lies and an accomplished deceiver. He is so good at deceit that he can conjure up evidence to prove his lie. He can tell us things that are not true so that we accept them as truth.

The Holy Spirit and I processed those truths, which led me to conclude that I might have memories of lies. The realization that lies were responsible for keeping me in bondage and depressed released the angst I'd carried around for years.

Memories are just that, but they are also in the past, which I cannot change, but better than that, history cannot hurt me today. Hanging onto painful memories which may or may not be true causes the present to be filled with despair.

Fast forward to today. My current counselor has used the truths I've learned in the last few years to bring me to a point where I can accept the healing God has wanted for me from the beginning. Most days, I experience the peace that can only come from an all-loving, all-powerful God.

Lately, I've been obsessed about a door I refuse to open. One that I want the Holy Spirit to open that door and clean out the room so my freedom in Christ can be complete.

She asked if I thought the Holy Spirit needed me to help Him clean out my muck. I understand that the answer to that is no, but I have to be the one to tell Him it's okay to go in.

Another paradigm-shifting statement: "What if I told you there is no door?"

Wow! No door? What a powerful statement. The Holy Spirit started downloading truth to me as we talked through this statement.

What did Jesus' sacrifice accomplish? He was the perfect answer to satisfy the judgment of a God who is so Holy that He cannot allow sin or be around sin. In only the way a supernatural God could do, He became man through His son Jesus Christ, to experience life in the flesh, just as we do, yet without sin. Jesus chose to give Himself to be crucified for our sins. He suffered all the punishment we deserve and paid the penalty with the separation from His Father and the ultimate death.

But it didn't end in death and defeat … instead, with the Power that God the Father gave to Jesus Christ, His son, He conquered death and rose to a new life and now sits on the throne on the right hand of God. It doesn't end there. Because of His ascension into heaven, He was able to send the Holy Spirit into the world.

When a person accepts Jesus as Savior, that person is recognized by God as being Holy and without sin. We have access to all of the power, the same power that raised Jesus from the dead. Immediately God, in the form of The Holy Spirit, comes into us, and He will never leave us without the ability to resist the enemy's lies.

More good news is that the sacrifice took for good. God has the power to forgive. He has already given that gift with Jesus' sacrifice. Our past, present, and future sins are forgiven.

So, if I have no sin, and I'm already healed from the past, how can there be a door that keeps back things I won't release? There is nothing to release except for the *illusions* of the enemy. Satan's *illusions* are so strong it takes discerning scrutiny to understand that what we see isn't real. We can tap into the wisdom of The Holy Spirit and know there is no door because we have been entirely cleansed to purity forever because of Jesus' sacrifice. When we say we have things that need to be cleaned out, we are saying Jesus wasn't powerful enough to accomplish what He set out to do.

Living in the flesh, we still do imperfect things. We don't have to accept that when we agree with God that it was wrong and release it to Him, we have the power to receive His love and ignore the beating the enemy tells us we deserve.

I realize I'm not hiding hurt, fear, bitterness, and unforgiveness; I'm listening to the enemy tell me I don't have the power to overcome. This lie causes me to see a door that doesn't exist, hiding a room that isn't there with secrets I don't have. It isn't a secret if someone knows, and God knows.

Revelation 12:9 (NAS)
9 And the great dragon was thrown down, the serpent of old who is called the devil and Satan, who deceives the whole world; he was thrown down to the earth, and his angels were thrown down with him

.

2 Corinthians 11:3 (NASB 1995)
3 But I am afraid that, as the serpent deceived Eve by his craftiness, your minds will be led astray from the simplicity and purity of devotion to Christ.

John 6:27 (NASB)
27 Do not work for the food which perishes, but for the food which endures to eternal life, which the Son of Man will give to you, for on Him the Father, God, has set His seal.

I search through the confusion
to find the way out of my illusion.
I go to family, pastors, and friends,
instruction books I read to no end.

Can I find the answer in a podcast?
Is there anything on the internet that will last?
The answers I seek are hidden right now.
I want to understand but I don't know how.

I concluded after searching all these years,
the lessons I learned came with tears.
I can choose from many paths.
I want the one that answers all I ask.

I know God is the one who starts us out
on a journey, to learn what His love is about.
He desires us to seek a relationship with Him.
Then uses the bond to help others look within.

I searched until the clarity is revealed.
The fallen world has His truth concealed.
I see and wonder why I never saw before.
There isn't, never has been or ever will be a door!

Take That Leap of Faith

For all kinds of reasons, I had a low threshold for trust. I've also been a believer since eight years old and learned that I could trust God. Those two opposite views were a source of contradictory living.

By the time I was an adult, I had tried to trust but usually ended up trusting the wrong people. I wanted to trust God, but I was always afraid He was the one who punished me when I was "bad," which was most of the time because I wasn't perfect.

I started getting acquainted with Jesus. I had to separate the Trinity so I wouldn't be afraid to get to know the Godhead. I've been relying on Jesus, having a hard time accepting God as a loving Father. Because of my relationship with my "brother" Jesus Christ, I made steps to go to the Father.

I had years of approaching God and had a setback before I took the last step to get to Him. After years of this back and forth, never quite getting to where I yearned to be, I learned something valuable. God wanted me to be comfortable with Him, and the last hurdle to cross had to be a leap of faith. There wasn't any more room to walk to Him; the path definitely fell short.

I've had many encouragers in my life who have helped me with learning to love My God. It all boiled down to believing in the truth, but ultimately, I had to leap. When I finally decided I could trust the Father enough to leap, I did. And guess what? He was right where He said He would be, and I was safely tucked into His arms.

<u>**Isaiah 49:4 (NLT)**</u>

4 I replied, "But my work seems so uselss! I have spent my strength for nothing and to no purpose. Yet I leave it all in the Lord's hand; I will trust God for my reward."

<u>**2 Corinthians 1:18-19 (NLT)**</u>

18 As surely as God is faithful, our word to you does not waver between "Yes" and "no." 19 For Jesus Christ, the Son of God, does not waver between "yes" and "no." He is the one whom Silas, Timothy, and I preached to you, and as God's ultimate "yes," He always does what He says.

I'm taking steps to get to You, God,
I want to see Your approval nod.
Each step I take gets me closer to You.
But suddenly, a step takes You from my view.

I've been confused for many nights,
thinking the next step will make it right.
Each time I lose sight of You
I have to rediscover what is true.

The many steps I 've taken time after time
are the same ones I thought I had left behind.
Once again, I thought I was almost there
I wanted to get to You somehow somewhere.

But today, I look again, and now I see
the same darkness I want to leave.
It won't go away or leave me alone
I hear the words "you have no home."

But my spirit inside urges me on.
He tells me I will find the place I belong.
So, step by step through the dark
I keep moving, looking for the spark.

One day I see the suffocating darkness,
the next day, I notice the dark is now dusk.
Another step, and now I see gray skies.
My spirit is lifting, for the dawn is nigh.

Now I see the sun burst out.
It's so beautiful; I want to shout.
But I don't – instead, I look to the Father
and tell Him I don't want to go any further.

I ask Him why is it I can never arrive
in His arms, no matter how hard I try?
His eyes are filled with compassion and love.
I remain because of the fear I can't get rid of.

My spirit tells me to look at the truth,
look at my past to find the proof
that we can trust our Savior and King.
And for us to see the good His love brings.

I want to take another step,
But I hear these words, "No, not yet."
That next step won't take you any closer.
If you continue, the day will be over.

Puzzled, I look at this Perfect Being
and ask Him to explain what he means.
He looks at me, and I feel cherished.
I know my God doesn't want me to perish.

Daughter – I want you to know the mystery
and the reason you get stuck in your misery.
The reason is you don't leap but take a step.
Please hear me and my words; please accept.

You always and forever take all of the steps
until that one you just don't get.
The times you suddenly lose sight
and you are again thrust back into the night.

It's because I don't want you to walk.
A step isn't what you need at all.
This is what I want you to do,
It's a leap of faith I need from you.

If you take this leap of faith
you will land in my arms and see my face.
But, daughter of mine, the next step you take
puts you in a circle you won't escape.

So don't move from the spot you are in
until you can lose your fear and when
You do; the leap of faith you take
will lead you fully into my grace.

Photo 106081513 @ Vrabelpeter1 / Dreamstime.com

October

God, I don't Understand
Psalm 91 – March 2022

Lord, I don't know how to interpret Psalm 91. I believe You rescue those who love You and trust You. But when David goes on to say plagues and disease will not touch us … these things do touch us. People who love and trust You get sick, get hurt, are hit with the plague. So, is David telling us or speaking to us in a metaphoric spiritual sense? He will keep disease and trauma of the spirit from touching us.

Whatever touches our body cannot harm our spirit.

Isaiah 40:31 (ESV)
31 But they who wait for the Lord shall renew their strength; they shall mount up with wings like eagles; they shall run and not be weary; they shall walk and not faint.
Psalm 91:3(NLT)
3 For He will rescue you from every trap and protect you from deadly disease.

Psalm 9:10 (NLT)
10 If you make the Lord your refuge, if you make the Most High your shelter, no evil will conquer you; no plague will come near your home.

My Father God in heaven,
I remember how much You've given.
You've shown through acts of kindness
just how much You cherish us.

Scattered throughout Your word
is vast wisdom that has endured
all through time and the ages
so that death is not our wages.

I see statements made throughout
and declarations, some even shout
that on the first glance I see
doesn't make sense to me.

Your word tells us You keep us safe.
Sickness will not flood our place.
You protect us from the bad,
so, we can escape the sad.

Yet God I witness every day
those who love you slip away.
Cancer strikes their body.
Pain and suffering we must embody.

How can I justify the hate?
And about the hard and harsh of today
when Your word tells me You keep us safe
as long as we stay in our place.

I can ask these questions all day long,
and even put them in a song.
I can use my valuable time
and try to understand Your mind.

But Lord and Savior who loves me so,
this place of doubt You never want me to go.
Your desire has always been
for my complete trust from beginning to end.

The total trust we put in You
is the ingredient that takes us through
our life in this fallen world
until our true heritage unfurls.

No matter what happens while here,
You hold us close and dear,
and one day before too long
we'll be exactly where we belong.

Understanding Is Not the Objective.
Psalm 91 August of 2022

I got up this morning and struggled awhile trying to think my way out of the unsettledness that infiltrated my morning. I turned on some worship music, even sang a song or two. I exercised a bit and fixed a decent breakfast. But I was in danger of going through this day in gloom.

Then, Holy Spirit's voice finally penetrated the dark thoughts of my mind and told me to sit down and begin to write. When I write, it's as if my spirit can bypass my imperfect self and begin to declare the truth.

Holy Spirit, I am believing a lie that I can't stop the turmoil inside.

I think I've heard you now – I am a daughter of the King. THERE IS NO TURMOIL. I'm free, I've been made whole, and God the Father sees me as perfect and unblemished. So, what does that mean?

I must say STOP to the liar and deceiver! I will not accept his lies because he has no power over me. I will only hear the words of my Father, My Daddy because my Daddy loves me. The darts and lies of the enemy will not touch me. I will not even receive a nick. All around me and my family may be destruction, but we will never be engulfed in the dark because the light of the Son surrounds us.

<u>**Psalm 91:4-7(NLT)**</u>

4 He will cover you with His feathers. He will shelter you with His wings. His faithful promises are your armor and protection. 5 Do not be afraid of the terrors of the night, nor the arrow that flies in the day. 6 Do not dread the disease that stalks in darkness, nor the disaster that strikes at midday. 7 Though a thousand fall at your side, though ten thousand are dying around you, these evils will not touch you.

Thank You God for being my Father.
I know that You take Your love farther,
Because I can even call you Daddy!
You seek an intimate relationship with me.

You've done all of the hard work to ensure
that I can be perfect, holy, and pure.
The only action of my own I must take
Is to agree with you and let go of the hate.

Thank You, my Savior, friend and brother!
Thank You for your willingness to endure
the punishment and condemnation
You suffered for me without hesitation.

Thank You, Holy Spirit, for being here
deep inside of me quietly, waiting to ensure
that the minute I ask for anything
You speak and answers into my life, bring.

Thank You to the trinity
for bringing us into unity
and giving us all of the goodness.
You want me to be blessed.

For a short time we are born into the world
for a specific purpose as You unfurl
the plan that was and has always been,
even since and before time began.

Thank You for the love You give
to Your children as we live
in a fallen world but safe.
In You we have a secure place.

My praise and worship fill my heart
loving You and accepting You in every part
of the life you have given to me.
Thank You for the knowledge that I am free.

Even when fire falls all around.
Even when evil and the hard times abound.
You keep me and my family safe
from the evil one, every day.

I'm here in this life.
Despite all the turmoil and strife
I will remain steadfast in Your love
until You take us to our new home above.

What About Job?

I read Job 19 this morning. Job isn't one of those books people generally choose as their favorite book.

Most people have heard about Job. He is one of those elusive well-known persons we take for granted. Statements like "patience of Job," "the plight of Job," and "The Lord gives, and the Lord takes away" are phrases from Job people quote in everyday life with no thought as to where they came from.

We understand that bad things happen to good people through no fault of their own. I understand and accept this, but what has me disconcerted by reading Job is the knowledge that God allows Satan to have his way with Christians for no apparent reason. True, He gives Satan parameters that must be followed, but still, He allows it and then backs away.

Then there are Job's friends. What made them turn into Job's judge instead of his comforter? How could they heap hot coals on his already tenuous position? I had a thought that seemed plausible. At the beginning of Job's story, we know how affluent he was and how much God blessed Job. Don't you wonder if people, including Job's friends, were envious of the high position Job had? They probably wondered why they couldn't share in some of his wealth.

Above all the others in wealth and position, this person was brought down to nothing. Do you suppose they were smug with their thoughts?

"Now, Job will finally know how it feels to live like us."

Maybe not these exact words, but there must have been some deep-seated satisfaction.

The next mystery his friends had to solve was go find a reason for Job's suffering. Why, you ask, was that important to them? Simple. They couldn't admit that suffering sometimes happens without a cause. Job had to have done something terrible to have been so devastated, and if they could get him to admit it, they would know how to prevent it. Realizing there isn't always a reason we can name takes away the illusion we have control of our lives.

Job 1:21 (NIV)
21 Naked I came from my mother's womb, and naked I will depart. The Lord gave and the Lord has taken away; may the name of the Lord be praised.

Job 38 1-2 (ESV)
1 Then the Lord answered Job out of the storm. He said,
2 who is this that darkens my counsel with words without knowledge?

Job 42:5-6 (ESV)
5 My ears had heard of you, but now my eyes have seen you.
6 Therefore, I despise myself and repent in dust and ashes.

The most challenging concept for me to grasp
is how little control of this life I have.
I can obey all the rules and laws
and love people everywhere without cause.

The logical thought is because I'm nice
and because Jesus paid the ultimate price
for sinful nature upon the cross,
I won't be devastated by a loss.

Job is not a comfortable book to read.
Without provocation, and most people agree,
hard times came into Job's life.
Suddenly his blessings turned into strife.

All of his friends and even his wife
tried to explain away the travesty of life.
They accused him of doing something bad,
thus the reason God took everything he had.

Job didn't agree with his friends,
and he told them so and didn't bend.
He didn't give in to the lies they told.
His insistence was quite bold.

Job never cursed God like his wife counseled.
He didn't know why hardship surrounded
him. His confession was honest to God.
Imagine how disillusioned he was.

Job reminded everyone who heard
about the times he observed
the rules and regulations and all he did right.
He was sure he didn't deserve this plight.

It must have seemed like an eternity
before God spoke to bring clarity
to the way Job looked at his troubles.
But God's explanation burst his bubble.

Instead of telling Job how sorry He was,
or admit that He was the cause
of the destruction and heartache in Job's life
to the extent that Job wished to die.

God took Job back to before time.
He reminded Job that God's creation was fine
and how He was the one who provided life
To everything on earth, low or high.

God asked Job if he understood God's plan
He developed even before time began.
All of God's majesty He pointed out
so Job understood he wasn't so devout.

Job was humbled and admitted to God
how low and finite he really was.
He admitted the arrogance in his heart
for taking credit for things, he had no part.

God approved of the response Job made,
He forgave him and gave him a new day.
God showed Job the extent of His grace
By restoring Job to a much better place.

I can question God all I want
and wonder why I can't see beyond
the heartache and sadness I've had all my life.
I know God will rescue me from my plight.

A Lesson from David's Life

What are your thoughts when you wake up in the mornings? Research has shown that the thoughts we have when we wake determine what kind of day we have. Of course, we have the free will to change the trajectory of the day whenever we want.

God showed me a passage in Psalm this morning during my quiet time that convinced me that I must be more intentional about my thoughts. Not just during the day, but the first thoughts of the day.

After I read ***Psalm 34:12,*** I had a yearning in my heart to be able to wake up with that much positive anticipation. I would like to wake up with the confidence of the beauty of each day.

In the middle of my yearning, the Holy Spirit gave me an image of David. I realized that David was one of those who woke up with a lust for life. David embraced life no matter what state he was in. He was anointed King but was on the run for thirteen years before he could declare his kingdom. Then while king, one of his sons chased him away from his throne. He won glorious battles, strayed into forbidden places, repented, and returned to the Lord's presence. His life was filled with ***living.***

Our most poignant worship and praise songs come from David's pen. He played vigorously, fought hard, cried with pain, fully mourned, hated completely, loved intensely, and worshipped with abandonment. He didn't shy away from living even when he was in despair.

I would do well to heed his example If I want to one day have a lust for life and can't wait for each day to come so I can behold the beauty. We can embrace the goodness and beauty of life only if we face the ugly and hardness simultaneously and give those up to our God.

Psalm 34:12 (MSG)
12 Who out there has a lust for life? Can't wait each day to come upon beauty.

I Thessalonians 5: 16-18 (MSG)
Be cheerful no matter what; pray all the time; thank God no matter what happens. This is the way God wants you, who belong to Christ Jesus, to live.

What keeps me from waking each day
fully expecting great things as I go my way?
Why don't I anticipate the beauty and good
of God's creation and wonders as I should?

He answered me when I took time for Him.
He said so much, where do I begin?
David was a man after God's heart.
At a young age God told him how to start.

David's words tell us how to have a full life
in the easy times, and even in our strife.
Can you imagine God's acknowledgment
of being anointed as king, facing harassment?

He ran from friends who became enemies,
but never once did he give into enmity.
I can honestly say my life is not like that.
When I was hurt, I just sat.

I didn't pursue God because of my fear.
I was isolated from those I held dear.
My Father in Heaven loves and cherishes me.
He wants to show me all of the beauty.

I should focus on His goodness and love.
He asks me to forget the hurt and rise above.
He wants me to be excited about today,
admiring the beauty along the way.

Dear Lord, as I lay down my head tonight
I pray for rest and sweet dreams so I might
wake up refreshed and excited about the day.
I want to see the beauty along the way.

Photo 160639720 @ Pavel Aliakseyeu / Dreamstime.com

November

God Is So Much More

There are moments when something I've been trying to grasp finally hits me. It is that ah-ha moment that changes my life. I sometimes wish I can hang onto that feeling, but it isn't the feeling I want to hang onto. It's the confidence that the feeling represents. The confidence that Christ is in me, and I am in Him. I don't have to try and do, and there isn't a ritual I have to go through to be able to be in Christ. I don't have to say a certain thing or think a certain way. I am Him and He is me.

I want to study the Word to know the Word so I can BE the Word. I don't want to teach the Word; I want to BE the Word. Then when someone wants to understand what I have that they don't, I want to be able to explain without teaching, because God is so much more than a lesson. Grace isn't permission to do whatever and then be forgiven. Grace is the purification of our consciousness.

We don't have to have a feeling to know God is with us. I don't want to only feel God. I want to know God so well, and be confident that He is with me, that I act like He is with me. I'm in love with Jesus. I am the light no matter where I go. My experience is not based on my feeling of Jesus, it is to know who I am. When I have such confidence that I have the same power of the Lord, that I don't have to do anything to call forth that power, I don't have to pray for the power to do something … I have the power to do something. I have the power to know, to be healed, to walk through adversity … not unscathed. Jesus was not unscathed, but I can walk through adversity intact.

God loves me. God made me for a relationship with Him. God gave me the power to stomp on hell wherever I go.

<u>I Peter 5:10 (ESV)</u> *And after you suffer a little while, the God of all grace, who has called you to His eternal glory in Christ, will Himself restore, confirm, strengthen, and establish you.*

<u>Ephesians 4:13 (ESF)</u>
13 Until we all attain to the unity of the faith and of the knowledge of the Son of God, to mature manhood, to the measure of the stature of the fullness of Christ.

Lord Jesus my Father and Savior,
how do I tell others how wonderful You are?
What words can I say to tell of your love?
What can I do to bring your love from above?

I need do nothing to make it happen.
When I accept You in my life, I can tap in.
Tap into the power You put in my life,
the power that can offset trouble and strife.

Lord, I want to be swayed by Your heart.
I don't want to be swayed by any part
of the lies the enemy has told me.
I want to be done with him and be free.

I want to know truth by Your mercy and grace.
Your truth is the reason I can face
anything I might experience at any time.
I will face the hurt but remain good and kind.

God, I love You more than I can know.
I love You more than I can show.
I want to tell others of the love You have,
and how you heal us with Your salve.

Accept the Compliment

I have a difficult time receiving a compliment. When I'm told I did a good job or look good, the words create an agonizing internal conflict between opposing forces.

I take pride in doing good things and doing them well. As a young girl, I loved affirmations. I wasn't very old when I learned that pride was something we should never have. It's a sign of selfishness and something that isn't pleasing to the Lord. Consequently, a compliment started a cycle in my soul, which caused me grief. I couldn't figure out how to appreciate kind words without being prideful.

I would do something good and receive praise for it, which gave me a warm fuzzy feeling. But alas, it didn't last long. The voice in my head said I only did good to be noticed and complimented, which is pride. I learned as a young person that pride is one of the unpardonable sins.

If I did terrible things, I would also be wrong. So, I have to keep doing good things. Then what happens when I get praised? I can't accept it because I am praised for doing good, and I only do good because I crave the affirmation, which is pride, and thus bad.

I know this resonates with someone because I cannot believe I am the first person to have experienced this constant tugging between two internal forces.

I had counsel from a wise person who reminded me of the greatest commandment confirmed by Jesus in Mark. We all know the verse, ***"Love the Lord ..."*** but how often do we consider the last part of His statement? ***"Love ... as you love yourself."***

God wants us to love our neighbors like we love ourselves. He didn't say love your neighbors, as I love your neighbors, or love your neighbors as I love you. Suppose we do not give ourselves or receive from others, nurturing, grace, encouragement, and compliments. How will we be able to treat our neighbors with regard?

Ecclesiastics 1:9 (NIV)
What has been will be again, what has been done will be done again; there is nothing new under the sun.

Romans 7:19 NIV)
19 For I do not do the good I want to do, but the evil I do not want to do—this I keep on doing.
Mark 12: 30-32 (NIV)
30 Love the Lord your God with all your heart and with all your soul and with all your mind and with all your strength.'[a] 31 The second is this: 'Love your neighbor as yourself.'[b] There is no commandment greater than these.

I like your hair, and you do good work.
I like to hear those words.
We call them compliments and the receiver
appreciates what they mean to her.

I ached for good words spoken over me.
I craved compliments, but you see,
I could not receive compliments at all,
The conflict caused my countenance to fall.

One day I was with my friend
someone complimented my complexion.
I hurtfully replied "as a matter of fact.
the reason my skin is smooth is that I am fat."

The look on the stranger's face caused me to stop.
She looked like a favorite balloon had popped.
I didn't stop but something changed inside.
I realized I had hurt her, and I wanted to hide.

I'm not the only one who doesn't know how
to accept compliments. We don't allow
kind words since we believe deep inside
praise will cause us to have pride.

We keep ourselves humble with our words.
When we do, negativity occurs.
We might as well call our encourager a liar,
which isn't the outcome either of us desires.

I read a statement made by Corrie Ten Boom.
She was honored at a banquet in a full room.
Everyone spoke of her in adoring terms.
The miracles of her survival were confirmed.

Ms. Ten Boom spoke to everyone there.
She showed wisdom because she cared.
"I accept these compliments. Let me propose
that each kind word spoken is a rose."

The audience sat still, waiting for more.
"I will regift this bouquet to One we adore.
He's the Good Father and God of all.
Only by God's grace am I standing tall."

When I'm complimented on something I do
I accept the words and believe they are true.
At the end of the day, I gather every rose,
give them to My Father my gratitude to show.

Where Is The Meaning?

I have lived many years, but the many years are nothing compared to eternity. The Bible often compares life to a flower; here today, gone tomorrow, or how to plan for a future that may not be available to us. We are taught to lay up treasures for ourselves, contrary to God's design.

The generation growing up in today's world was planned by God from before time began. This generation has grown up in a dark time when right is wrong, and wrong is right. We have gender confusion and don't understand the definition of marriage. I pray that parents of this generation lead their children to become mighty warriors for the kingdom. I pray they will praise and worship our God with abandonment as we let His light shine through us in this dark world. I pray for boldness to confess the Lord God as Savior and King. May this generation understand what the true meaning of life is, and may they learn to walk in the Spirit and not the flesh.

Galatians 5:13-14 (ESV)
13 For you were called to freedom, brothers. Only do not use your freedom as an opportunity for the flesh, but through love serve one another. 14 For the whole law is fulfilled in one word: "You shall love your neighbor as yourself."

Colossians 3:23-24 (ESV)
23 Whatever you do, work heartily, as for the Lord and not for men, 24 knowing that from the Lord you will receive the inheritance as your reward. You are serving the Lord Christ.

I want to leave my body and be free.
I'm tired of gravity limiting what I see.
I want to float high above,
higher and farther than even a dove.

If I could shed this flesh of mine
and escape into a land with no time
I think my joy would be complete.
I wouldn't care if I had nothing to keep.

Maybe one day when the Father says
it's time to finally take His children away.
Perhaps on that day, I can finally be
rescued from all the ugly and be free.

But until that day comes, I must remain
and take the time and energy to refrain
from wanting to escape my life
and somehow see beyond the strife.

I must recognize the good
and be joyful and happy like I should.
The only way that can ever be
is to ignore my flesh and let my spirit free.

How can I ignore my flesh, so solid,
something that is so here but squalid.
How can we watch as Life unfurls?
The mystery of the goodness of God.

is something that cannot be understood at all.
He's bigger than everything,
and He decides what our life will bring.
We live in such a finite state,

here one minute, and the next, it's too late
to do all of the things we had planned
because we ran out of time.
Only God knows the length of our days.

Only God knows when we go or stay.
It doesn't matter how hard I wish
God is the only one who can truly finish.

Looking Beyond Grief

Grief is like Texas weather. In any given week, we can experience the gamut of weather. Clouds, rains, and storms give way to beautiful crisp mornings full of birds singing and sunshine. Then suddenly, we experience gray, gloomy stifling humidity. On the same day, the weather turns to spring with flowers blooming. Spring weather gives way to a windy, desolate cry of nature, rain intermingled with the screams and protest of thunder until all emotions are spent. The world slowly returns to a milder existence with soft winds, still cloudy but with some sun. The rain has ended because all of the tears are gone. There remains a chill over mother nature's soul because of the emotions' aftermath.

I often compare nature to my feelings because, so often, it mirrors my emotions. God is above all because the indisputable fact is that God created all. I don't think that is by accident. God created nature for humankind to live in harmony. One cannot be whole without the other. Adam and Eve's sin disrupted the peace, and we have been trying to correct the imbalance.

Loss is a constant in our minds. How many times does grief so consume us that we can't remember who we really are? As we go through the days of mourning, it is essential to remember that grief is not our identity!

The Word of God has a message of hope because it tells us that no matter what has happened in our lives, the one constant that never changes is God the Father. Our identity remains solid and unbending. Through Christ, we have access to all power, all mercy, all hope, and all joy. During our days of grieving, we can choose to renew and explore what it means to be us, a child of the King.

Our loved ones can never be replaced, and there is a vacuum because of their departure, but we have a choice with what we fill that vacuum. God wants to be the one to fill the emptiness with Himself, the God of Love. If He doesn't fill the void, the enemy will take up residency and fill it with sorrow, anger, bitterness, despair, and disunion.

Galatians 3:26-28 (NIV)

26 So in Christ Jesus you are all children of God through, 27 For all of you who were baptized into Christ have clothed yourselves with Christ. 28 There is neither Jew nor Gentile, neither slave nor free, nor is there male and female for you are all one in Christ Jesus.

James 1:2-4 (NIV)

2 Consider it pure joy, my brothers and sisters, whenever you face trials of many kinds, 3 because you know that the testing of your faith produces perseverance. 4 Let perseverance finish its work so that you may be mature and complete, not lacking anything.

I look through the eyes of the disheartened,
those whose loved ones have departed,
and see a season of intense grief,
days filled with despair showing no relief.

I understand the sadness and despair
and the angry feelings that life isn't fair.
I've had my share of tragedy and trauma
Living through abuse and intense drama.

We know we will see the world as before
because of a God who will restore
us to the wholeness, the intent he had in mind
when He decided to create humankind.

Sin destroyed the purity of God's creation,
but, He already planned for our salvation.
If anyone sincerely and willingly believes,
God's only Son suffered so we could be free.

The beauty of the Father is this …
He pursues us and guides those that are His.
Wherever we wander or how far we go
He is ready, His grace and guidance to show.

Before I embraced the goodness of God
The world was dark and everyone, a fraud.
I couldn't accept any redeeming qualities.
My eyes were clouded, and I couldn't see.

For years I wanted to find the peace
the word of God promised He would release.
I desired the confidence to finally stop
my anxiety and find a better way to adopt.

The answer to our anxiety and fear
is the same as when we've lost someone dear.
Look to the Father for our comfort and peace.
The power of the Holy Spirit will be released.

Dear Father, thank You for the goodness
of your nature. Holy Spirit, don't let us miss
out on the love of an awesome
God, as the joy in our soul blossoms.

Photo 27903822 @ Zaretskaya / Dreamstime.com

December

Stay In Your Lane

When I was young, the churches I attended emphasized getting lost souls into the church. The premise was once they were within the church's walls, the Holy Spirit would have a better chance of helping them get converted.

I didn't have a problem with the concept. What always made me uncomfortable was the "bribes" they created to get them in the doors. I always thought that Jesus is rewarding enough as He is. Why do we feel we must window dress Him for the world to accept Him?

When we are passionate about God's love for us and what He did through His Son Jesus Christ, with the help of the Holy Spirit, others will want to know what we have. The Holy Spirit is the one who draws people to the Father, and He can and will use our enthusiasm for the kingdom to do it. He doesn't **need** us, but He loves to partner with us.

I've discovered something else about myself regarding God's design for my life. For years I looked for my worth and what I was supposed to do by comparing myself with what others did. If I thought what they were doing was intriguing, I made it my goal to do the same without considering what talents the Father gave me.

Sadly, I never did achieve my goal if it wasn't in God's plan. At the same time I was pursuing someone else's job, the work which God had for me went dormant.

God has a plan for each of us. He gives us the tools and talents to accomplish His goal. If we could stop trying to walk on someone else's path, we would get to the end result more effortlessly and faster. I stay in my lane by listening to the instructions from The Holy Spirit and keeping my eyes off others' lives.

<u>**Jeremiah 29:11 (NIV)**</u>
11 "For I know the plans I have for you," declares the Lord, "plans to prosper you and not to harm you, plans to give you hope and a future."

<u>**2 Kings 14:10 (NASB)**</u>
10 You have indeed defeated Edom, and your heart has become proud. Enjoy your glory and stay at home; for why should you provoke trouble so that you, even you, would fall, and Judah with you.

<u>**John 21:20-23 (MSG)**</u>
Turning his head, Peter noticed the disciple Jesus loved following right behind. When Peter noticed him, he asked Jesus, "Master, what's going to happen to him?" 22 Jesus said, "If I want him to live until I come again, what's that to you? You – follow me."

Consider the Gospel and what it means.
Is it something we say or something seen?
The scriptures we read, the sermons we hear,
lessons to which we are taught to adhere.

All these things prompt us to figure ways
to make salvation palpable to amaze
the world about the greatness of God,
and how to receive His approval nod.

The truth is much more simplistic, you see.
We must believe that God set us free
from the wages of sin, which is God's wrath
and the finality of God's Judgment of death.

We don't have to work hard or strive
To convince others of a better way of life.
The Gospel is mighty and great enough,
sharing with others isn't all that tough.

When we willingly open ourselves up
to the Holy Spirit and allow Him to engulf us,
He infuses His energy into our will
and bestows His wisdom until we are filled.

God created us with the proper tools
to become what He planned for us to do.
Our curiosity, foolishness, and pride
led us to investigate the other side.

Our focus shifted to our discovery there,
and our desires determined life isn't fair
because God didn't give us the advantages.
We craved those and ignored what was for us!

In ignorance, we adhere to our great desire
to design a plan to allow us to go higher.
For a time, we may succeed,
but before long we wallowed in our greed.

Greed moves us into a world of competition,
into which we entered with no hesitation.
In the end, no matter how hard we try,
our accomplishments only leave us dry.

God doesn't want us to travel another path.
He didn't give us energy into which to tap.
We detoured into a plan for someone else.
We became exhausted and devoid of success.

Unless we get back to God's plan for our life,
our days are filled with turmoil and strife
of endlessly working someone else's job
while our work is not done, our joy is robbed.

Take heart if this has happened to you.
Seek the Father, and He will set your feet true
to do the tasks with what He provides
and do the job in which you can take pride.

It isn't for others to dictate our skills
or talents or determination of God's will.
God has a specific plan for you and me.
As we rest in His wisdom, our souls are free.

The Logic of Reasoning

I like order and predictability. I think with my left brain. I adhere to the concept that logic dictates if we care to have an orderly universe. But let me break it down into a more personal statement. If my life is to be orderly, what I perceive, I must be able to logically justify.

I am also a believer. I accepted Jesus Christ as my savior as a young girl. Reconciling beliefs and logic isn't so complicated while we are young. I found that the more I learned about the world, the more I had to grow my faith. Though I'm not sure I am the one to increase my faith, I'll go with that thought.

The more I learned about the Trinity and the nature of our Heavenly Father, the more distraught I became. I realized I could no longer rely on logic to understand life and keep my world orderly.

Recently, the Holy Spirit has been urging me to let go of my expectations regarding who God is. We don't have the mind of God, and we will never know the depth or the width of Him. Those concepts mean I cannot rely on logic to help me figure out my world. It means I can no longer reason out God's plan or how He will accomplish His will for my life.

God's idea of order is not mine. What does all of this mean? It means that if I live according to God's word, I must go to Him to show me His way. The Holy Spirit is God in us. We can know Him because Jesus Christ completed His mission, His death, resurrection, and His ascension back to the Father.

Relying on the Holy Spirit means I no longer obsess with logic and the ability to reason things out. The more I learn of His nature, the more peace, confidence, security, and contentment I have. That, my dear sojourners, means more freedom to just be.

<u>**Numbers 23:19 (ESV)**</u>
19 God is not man, that He should lie, or a son of man that He should change His mind. Has He ever spoken and failed to act? Has He ever promised and not carried it through?

<u>**Isaiah 40:28 (NLT)**</u>
28 Have you never heard? Have you never understood? The Lord is the everlasting God, the Creator of all the earth. He never grows weak or weary. No one can measure the depths of His understanding.

I said these words many times in my life,
"God explain the wheres or whys.
Show me if this is what you want me to do.
If it doesn't make sense, I will refuse.

"I pray for Your wisdom to help me see
if what I hear is You telling me.
Please validate what my thoughts are saying,
I can't understand, then I am staying."

I go back and forth, and make a list
of the pros and cons, so I don't forget.
If I think this all through long enough
I can finally figure out why life is tough.

I sit down, take a pen, and write out
the truths of God that I can never doubt.
One item God keeps saying and it is above
anything else because it's about His love.

The questions I ask of myself are not right.
Instead, I should ask Him to help me fight.
My mind fights doubts and confusion
because I keep looking for a good reason.

God is not logical, and doesn't make sense.
So why must I keep straddling the fence?
He wants me to take some kind of action,
be it wrong, be it right. It matters not to Him.

As long as His character isn't defiled.
He protects us like a parent does a child.
Think of your children and how they act.
They rush head on without thinking to ask.

When they are doing something wrong,
don't say they are bad and they don't belong.
The plan is to teach them how to discern
where the Father wants us to go to learn.

Let's teach our children to do the right thing,
so when they grow into adults, they bring
comfort and encouragement for others,
taught to them by fathers and mothers.

They don't try to reason and logically think
about how to be good or the right thing.
God has the same idea for me and for you.
Don't use logic. He has something for you.

Listen to your spirit and do as He directs.
His plan won't be what you expect.

Live In The Spirit
Romans 8:1-39

What does it mean to live in the Spirit? I've been intrigued by the Holy Spirit concept and its relation to real life and our existence. I've searched Scripture, meditated with the Father, and compiled all I've been taught by Bible scholars more versed in the Word than I. I have concluded that my flesh cannot understand the ways of the Spirit. My flesh is conceived with sin attached. My Spirit is from God because, in the beginning, God breathed His very breath into Adam (then Eve), which is Spirit.

God created us as spiritual beings so He can commune with us intimately in the only way He can, in our Spirit. The beauty is that He left His throne in Heaven, took the form of man, and walked in the limitations of the flesh so He could understand what it looked and felt like to be us living in a fallen world. Sacrificing his Kingship allowed Him to know what we face daily, so He can better relate with us. Our God understands what we feel, and He can comfort and encourage us in our walk until that day we are with Him in our Spirit forever.

We have difficulty here and now because the world caters to the flesh and Satan is the prince of the heavens. The enemy can, and he does, do his best to keep us in bondage. His purpose is to cause as much chaos and unrest in this world as possible. It is our responsibility to let Holy Spirit be in control of us.

Romans 8:1-4 (NLT)

1 So now there is no condemnation for those who belong to Christ Jesus 2 And because you belong to him, the power of the life-giving Spirit has freed you from the power of sin that leads to death. 3 The law of Moses was unable to save us because of the weakness of our sinful nature. So God did what the law could not do. He sent his own Son in a body like the bodies we sinners have. And in that body God declared an end to sin's control over us by giving his Son as a sacrifice for our sins. 4 He did this so that the just requirement of the law would be fully satisfied for us, who no longer follow our sinful nature but instead follow the Spirit.

Romans 8:7-8 (NLT)

7 For the sinful nature is always hostile to God. It never did obey God's laws, and it never will. 8 That's why those who are still under the control of their sinful nature can never please God.

Romans 8:38-39 (NLT)

38 And I am convinced that nothing can ever separate us from God's love. Neither death nor life, neither angels nor demons, neither our fears for today nor our worries about tomorrow—not even the powers of hell can separate us from God's love. 39 No power in the sky above or in the earth below—indeed, nothing in all creation will ever be able to separate us from the love of God that is revealed in Christ Jesus our Lord.

My Savior, my God, is my salvation.
I need not give in to the world's expectations.
Though I am in this world right now
the Holy Spirit fills me with His power.

Christ sacrificed Himself, so I am saved.
The power that rose Christ from the grave
is the same power that resides in my spirit.
He freely gives His love, I won't reject it.

Father – Abba – God, I receive and agree
that my spirit is awakened and set free.
Your grace keeps me from sin.
I need never allow my flesh victory again.

I rejoice in the greatness of my Savior.
Because of His love, I have found favor.
I will learn to walk where he guides me,
and with expectation, I await my Jubilee.

There Is Beauty in Imperfection

I read those words, and my soul rebelled. NO! How can there be beauty in imperfection? I spent my entire life looking for perfection, for ways to be more perfect. I learned at an early age that if I could find the perfect will of God, I could have life and have it more abundantly. In my pursuit of perfection, I determined that life abundantly meant a life of peace, tranquility, and absence of trauma and pain.

Reality is relative, and perception is individual. These are the truths I've learned in my pursuit to understand this complicated existence called life. I've watched enough Science Fiction movies and read enough twisted novels to recognize how easy it is to phase into a different reality. With one temporally disruptive phase, one slingshot around the sun, or one jump in the universe and life can be entirely backward.

Have you experienced a reality where people start out as adults and gradually "grow" into children until the end of life appears to be the beginning? No? Does that mean it doesn't exist? Do you believe there is another dimension parallel to our existence; an entire society is walking our path but experiencing situations in an opposite perception?

What about those who we have determined are mentally ill? Might they have been displaced from their reality and dimension into ours where what we decide is normal is entirely out of phase with their idea of normal? How would we feel if we were thrust into a reality where the same people and places exist but live at night and sleep in the day? What would that look like?

Consider this. If we strive for perfection, how will we know when perfection has been conquered? Your idea of perfection might be my idea of complete failure. We can't even choose a group of people to represent us because how can we find a group with the same ideals and desires? Of course, all of us share characteristics, but at different levels. Even cloning wouldn't produce sameness. God has created such complex creatures that we may duplicate some parts, but how does one copy a soul?

It is the uniqueness of each other that attracts us. It is the variety that keeps us interested in what's around the bend, and it is the unknown that keeps us searching. Let us embrace our imperfections or differences and strive to understand what it means to care about each other.

Ecclesiastes 3:11 NASB)
11 He has made everything appropriate in its time. He has also set eternity in their heart, without the possibility that mankind will find out the work which God has done from the beginning even to the end.

1 Corinthians 8:2 ((NLT)
2 Anyone who claims to know all the answers doesn't really know very much.

I believed perfection was the standard.
But, perfection cannot be planned
unless we compare our perfection to the truth,
which only comes from He who rules.

God is the standard of perfection to be used.
Our idea of perfection is confused,
because we compare ideas with each other.
Perfection is a fallacy we discovered.

Perception helps us understand our world.
An individual life has a mystery to unfurl.
Don't leave out the critical component
of whom we choose for our proponent.

I often asked a teacher, preacher, or friend
what I must do to live a life of perfection.
The conclusion I came to was it was all folly.
We have different ideas. I can rely on nobody.

God made a unique way.
A manner in which we can be saved.
Our faith and trust in Jesus Christ, our Lord
is the way to perfection. It's in His Word.

God conceived each one of us uniquely,
and He loves us completely.
Whether we are perfect in this life or not
He accepts us because of what He bought.

Jesus Christ came and lived as one of us
and He lived without sin.
Christ sacrificed Himself for the atonement
God requires. We need not be despondent.

The imperfection each of us represents
lets us celebrate life and prevents
a world of boredom caused by sameness
and our ideas of what perfection is.

Bibliography

<u>Amplified Bible (AB)</u>
Scripture quotations marked (AB) are taken from The Amplified Bible, New Testament,
Copyright@1954, 1958, 1987, by the Lockman Foundation. Used by permission. All rights reserved.

<u>English Standard Version (ESV)</u>
Scripture quotations marked "ESV" are taken from The Holy Bible, English Standard Version.
Copyright @ 2000;2001 by Crossway Bibles, a division of Good News Publishers.
Use by permission. All rights reserved.

<u>The Message (MSG)</u>
Scripture quotations from The Message,
Copyright @ by Eugene H. Peterson 1993, 1994, 1995, 1996, 2000, 2001, 2002.
Used by permission of NavPress Publishing Group. All rights reserved.

<u>New American Standard Bible (NASB)</u>
Scripture taken from the New American Standard Bible
Copyright @ 1960, 41962, 1963, 1986, 1971, 1972, 1975, 1977, 1995, by Lockman Foundation
Used by permission. All rights reserved.

<u>New Living Translation (NLT)</u>
Scripture quotations marked (NLT) are taken from the Holy Bible, New Living Translation,
Copyright @ 1996.
Used by permission of Tyndale House Publishers, Inc., Wheaton, IL 60189 USA. All rights reserved.

<u>New King JamesVersion (NKJV)</u>
Scripture quotations marked "NKJV" are taken from the New King James Version.
Copyright @ 1982 by Thomas Nelson, Inc.
Used by permission. All rights reserved.

Roxanne Gail Hodge uses her wisdom and vast experience to write inspirational books, novels, and poetry to entertain, and inspire hope. Her walk with the Lord has been her solace while surviving many of the worst life-changing events. Through His Strength, she didn't just survive, she overcame. Roxanne has two daughters and four grandchildren who reside in Texas. Her passions are writing thrillers, poetry, short stories, reading, retrospection, and painting.

THE LONG ROAD BACK, a thrill-seeking suspense novel, was published in 2019. With much success, the second edition of her novel was released in the winter of 2020. Her readers loved the characters so much they requested a sequel. Thus was born *BENEATH THE GLITTER,* an FBI thriller about human trafficking, released June of 2022.

Roxanne has spent her entire life journaling both poetry and poetic words. She accumulated some of her favorite life-altering poetry and created a one-of-a-kind systemic view of her own life in her own words. This poetry book reveals profoundly heartwarming events throughout Roxanne's life to enlighten the truth that all things are possible through God. *THISTLES AND BLOSSOMS* released in the Fall of 2020.